THE LARGEST SELLERS ON EBAY.COM

FIGURES - DATA - FACTS

Marion von Kuczkowski

Imprint
Marion von Kuczkowski
Contact: mvk@tmta.de
Website: www.take-me-to-auction.de
Translator: Ginger Kern
Cover Design: © fotomek - Fotolia.com

ISBN-13: 978-1503148611
ISBN-10: 1503148610

Contents

Foreword

Aside from time and experience, an outstanding market knowledge and marketplace knowledge are among the pillars needed to build a successful eBay business.

In "The Largest Sellers on eBay.com" I have analyzed the listings of more than a hundred eBay.com Titanium Power Sellers* while evaluations provide answers to the questions that every seller that sells on eBay.com should be asking, such as:

- On what days are the most items sold on eBay.com and what days see the highest sale prices?
- Which listing duration period has proven itself to be the best in terms of selling price and sales quota?
- What is the average selling price of the items sold on eBay.com?
- What is the proportion of auctions among the listing formats available to sellers?

Which are the bestsellers among the eBay sellers with the highest revenues, and which are the bestsellers among the sellers with the highest sales figures?

In "The Largest Sellers on eBay.com," you will find out what the numbers look like for the High Volume eBay sellers and get ideas on how to improve your own eBay listings.

A successful eBay business can't be built overnight. Established eBay businesses have the advantage that they have already invested a lot of time and gained experience, but they have also started from scratch and work every day to meet the needs and requirements of the dynamic eBay marketplace.

The evaluations in this book show that there is potential for optimization, even for the top eBay sellers, and that ambitious newcomers still have opportunities to start on eBay.

*Titanium Power Sellers must generate at least $1,800,000 in sales or sell 180,000 items per year.

Introduction

eBay was founded in 1995 by Pierre Omidyar and since its inception 19 years ago, it has developed into a gigantic revenue generating machine. Hundreds of thousands of sellers around the world compete for their livelihood by selling on eBay.

After I analyzed the German eBay sales millionaires, I followed it with an analysis of High Volume sellers who are active on the US marketplace. Unlike in the first German version, in which I only analyzed sellers located in Germany, in the evaluation of US sellers I deliberately avoided confining the analysis to the location because, as you will see later, sellers mainly from Asia represent a marketplace power on eBay.com that should not be underestimated.

Originally, I wanted to find 50 sellers whose monthly sales were each between $500,000 and $1,000,000, plus 50 sellers that generated revenue of at least $1 million on eBay.com, plus 50 sellers that sold at least 30,000 items per month on eBay.com.

All these sellers fulfill eBay's requirements for the "Titanium Power Seller" status.

To get the "Titanium Power Seller" status on eBay.com, the sellers must have a minimum revenue of $1.8 million per year, or complete 180,000 transactions per year.

After I analyzed the sales of hundreds of the eBay sellers that I decided upon at the beginning, a total of 158 sellers remained from the three groups. I didn't want to leave any of these sellers out, so I have included all 158 in the analysis.

52 sellers belong to group 1, the group whose monthly sales generated between $500,000 and $1,000,000 on eBay.com. Group 2, the group of sellers that generated revenues of at least $1,000,000 per month on eBay.com, includes 54 sellers.

Group 3, the group of sellers selling at least 30,000 items on eBay.com per month, also includes 52 sellers.

In this third group, there are 15 sellers that already appear in groups 1 and 2, but I did not want to exclude them because in the evaluations, the groups are appraised individually and had I excluded the 15 sellers that generated more than $500,000 in sales on eBay.com, the results of group 3 would have been misrepresented.

In analyses involving all three groups, I have calculated these 15 sellers only once so that the results are correct. Therefore, we'll evaluate 143 sellers overall.

The data points were collected between mid-June 2014 and the end of July 2014, where each seller was analyzed for exactly 30 days.

This analysis is a snapshot that refers to the evaluated period. Seasonal variations are quite possible, so some sellers, like the ones selling pools and accessories for example, could be assigned to individual groups during the period of analysis, even though they would likely not rank at all on the lists during the winter months. In winter, sellers that specialize in fireplaces, for example, would pop up on the lists instead, not having obtained a place on the list in summer.

To give you a taste of the data analyzed, I would like to start with some impressive numbers: the 143 sellers analyzed have sold 3,510,854 items and generated an incredible $163,398,705 in revenue within just 30 days. Together they have a total of 46,663,144 ratings.

Overall, they fill the eBay marketplace with 5,095,498 listings, including a total of 306,847,127 items.

In 30 days they have received 7,878,099 bids.

Read on to learn what the numbers of the eBay High Volume Sellers look like. Learn how many items they post on eBay.com and how many they sell successfully, when they started on eBay.com, and what countries they are located in.

See which listing formats are used most often and on which days the sellers achieve the highest prices or the highest sales quotas. You will also learn which times acquire the highest prices or the highest sales quotas and which items belong to the list of bestsellers among the sellers analyzed.

Clare Gilmartin, Vice President of eBay Marketplaces, once said that 38% of sales are generated by a small number of eBay sellers [1]. At the sales volume that the analyzed sellers combine to reach, it can be assumed that the results of the analysis reflect the overall situation on eBay.com's marketplace and that the data analyzed thus provides answers to many questions like, for example, what day is the best day to sell on eBay.com or which listing durations have proven themselves successful.

This book is intended for experienced eBay sellers. You will not find a step-by-step guide to starting successfully on eBay in this book, yet the secrets of eBay Power Sellers will be revealed. My goal was to analyze the figures, data and facts from eBay.com Titanium Sellers and to provide a clear representation thereof.

Before we get to the final analysis, I would like to note that I would have preferred to have represented the data of each of the three groups in differently colored images. Unfortunately, the print version of this book would have cost over $20 with color graphics and since some of the older e-book readers can't display color graphics, I decided against this option and made one image each per group.

Sellers analyzed

The following sellers were analyzed in the three individual groups - the order is alphabetical:

Group 1: between $500,000-$1,000,000 in revenue	Group 2: more than $1,000,000 in revenue	Group 3: more than 30,000 items sold
2ndswing	6ave	01cnyw2010
3ballsgolf	adoramacamera	accecity2009
a1_superdeals	altatac	alice1101983
accmonster	am-autoparts	altatac
allnewshop	apmex	am-autoparts
baltisales	apparelsave	apparelsave
betterworldbooks	asavings	beadofamerica
brand_jfa	audiosavings	bellaandchloe
budgetgolfer	beachcamera	bellaandchloe-2
cametaauctions	beckertime	betterworldbooks
centsles	best_buy	bhfo
cpo-outlets	bestchoiceproducts	blowitoutahere
diamond_jewelry_united	bhfo	bmw-yyh
doverjewelry	bidadoo_business	burbanksportscards
echefshop	bidallies	buy
factorydirectsale	blinq	campus111
garage_cell	blutek	carpartswholesale
gearxs	buy	chayatech
giftcardmall	buydig	city-green
globalgolf	buysuperdeal	cnazhi2012
golfetail	campus111	ecop!
gonitrohobbies	carpartswholesale	eforcity
greatbrands	certified-jewelry	elec-mall
hi-etech	chubbiestech	emilyandlily
k2motor	dailysteals	eroute66
ksouth9	deal.fisher	estocks_usa
manufacturer_certified	digjungle	gadgetstop
maxtoolsales	drivengps	gohastings

music123	ecop!	hi-etech
nps	emrude11	hkpowershop
nri-industrial	factory_outlet	hottestdealever
omnimodels	gadgetfix	jewelry-sale
poolproducts.com	gazelle-shop	lilyyangshop
poolsupplyworld	getitdigital	moviemars
reliableaftermarketpartsinc	jomashop	newegg
retailfashionoutlet	linda*s***stuff	phoenix1900
saveonpoolsupplies	mcm	planet_wireless
scottsdalesilver	newegg	qwb9876533
shopcelldeals	overstock	rrd20077
shopdivvy	photovideo4less	save_good
targetshops	prewarcardcollector	seemmy999
tee2green6931	proaudiostar	shcfshop
thewatchery	probstein123	tavses
threerb	quickshipelectronics	topgembead
wayfair	redchairdiamonds	zhangyunice
unique_squared_inc	redtagcamera	verabradley
unitedoutdoors	robertscamera	vminnovations
unlocked_nocontract	sflmaven	xtremegems2010
unlocked_nottobetied	silvertownelp	yallstock
verabradley	taddwholesale	yallshop
www-sonicelectronix-com	valuemassage	zorotools
yallshop	vminnovations	zydistro
	youbuyrite	
	zorotools	

In groups 1 and 2 there is some overlap with group 3, as noted above.

15 of the sellers listed in group 3 had a revenue of more than $500,000 during the analysis period and sold more than 30,000 items per month.

Since all groups have also been evaluated individually, I've taken these overlaps into account.

In the evaluations, which include the groups 1-3, I only incorporated these sellers into the calculation once.

Newcomers or veterans?

In groups 1 and 2 there are three sellers that have been around since 1998. Almost 53% of the sellers have already been registered with eBay for more than ten years, though that does not necessarily mean that they were active as eBay sellers for just as long or throughout that whole time period.

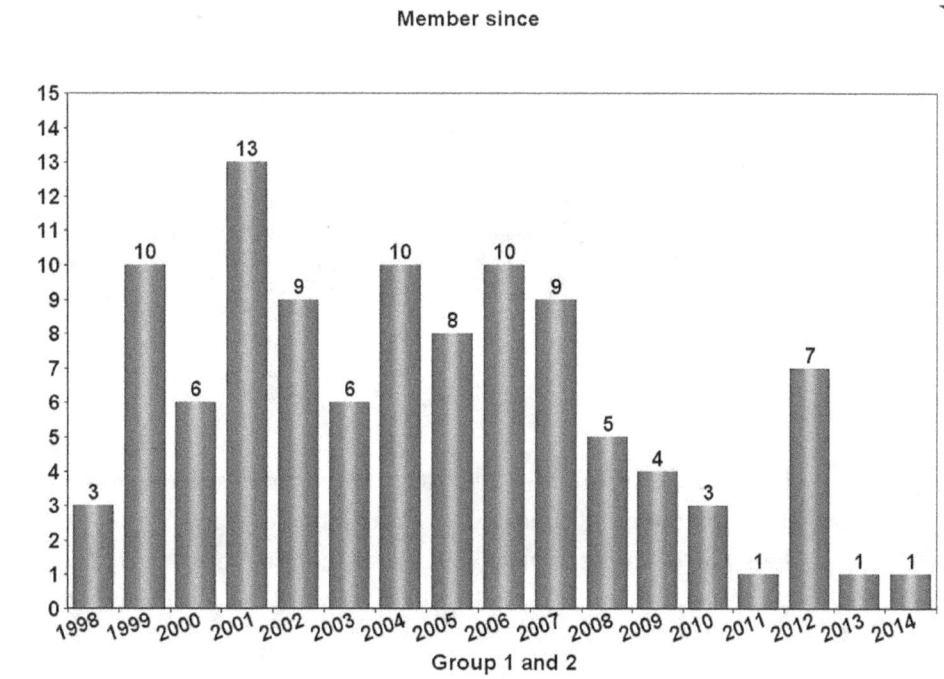

It is amazing that two newcomers can be found amongst the eBay sales millionaires.

One seller entered just this year and is already one of the eBay sales millionaires, while another is still quite new to eBay, having been a member for only one year.

A small peak in registration occurred in 2001, while sellers who registered on eBay after 2007 are represented less frequently in the group of sales millionaires, which does not mean that eBay was suffering from dwindling registrations.

The figures shown from group 3:

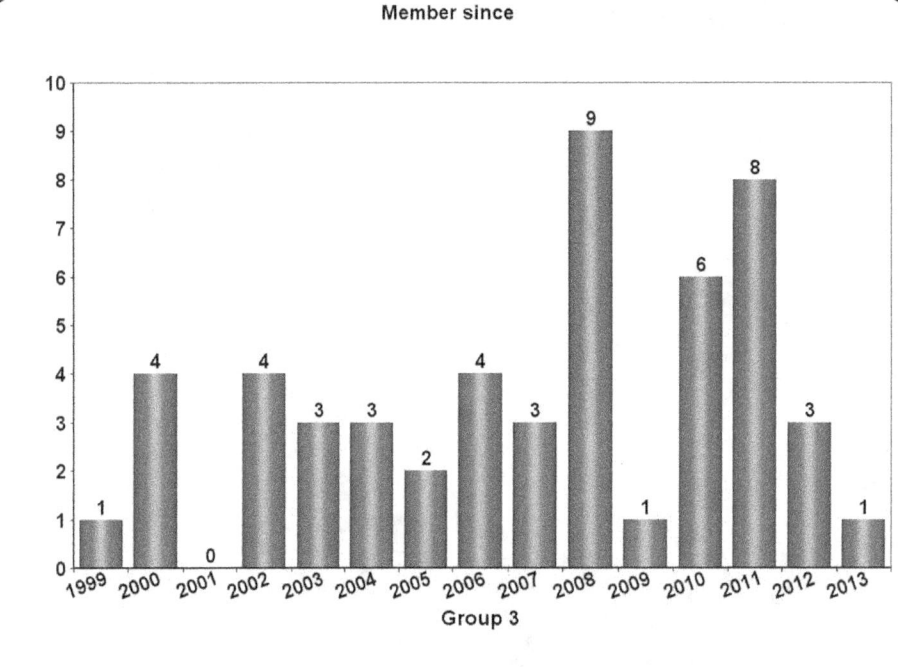

Member since

Group 3

Here it becomes clear that it is apparently easier to get to the top of sellers who sell many products in a relatively short amount of time than to break into the league of sales millionaires.

In the group of sellers who sell more than 30,000 items a month, more than 71% of them have been around for less than ten years, and almost 36% have been around for less than five years.

Feedback scores

Feedback scores are a popular topic on eBay. Sellers that break the magic barrier of more than 1,000,000 ratings are celebrated around the world and all sellers are very proud when their star's color changes.

The number of feedback ratings clearly plays an important role for many sellers, and also for buyers on eBay.

Even though most commercial sellers know that the sheer number of ratings says nothing about the success of a seller - I could sell 1 million products with a profit of $1 each and I would still be better off if I sold 100,000 products with a profit of $11 each - the question about the number of feedback ratings does often come up in conversations amongst sellers.

So let's take a look at the feedback scores of our three groups.

Overall, the 143 sellers in groups 1-3 we analyzed on eBay have almost 47 million feedback scores of which nearly 12 million feedback scores were in group 1, nearly 17.5 million feedback scores in group 2 and almost 31.5 million feedback scores in group 3 (14 million feedback scores of which must be subtracted from the overview, as they were already counted in groups 1 and 2).

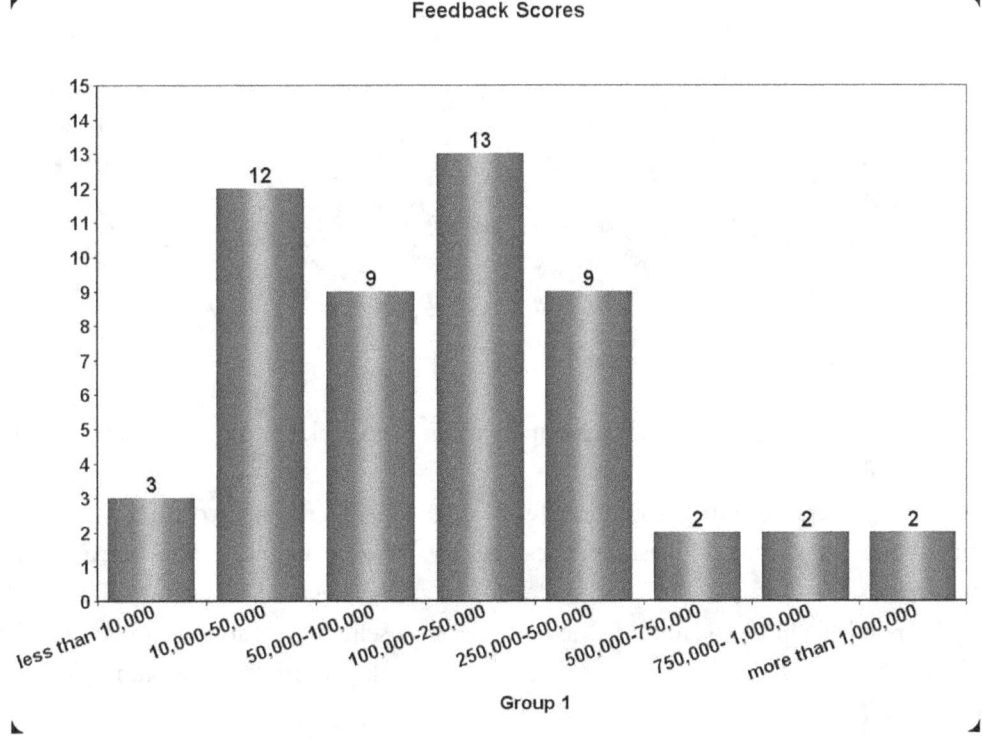

In group 1, the group of sellers who made between $500,000 to $1 million in revenue per month, most sellers had between 100,000 and 250,000 feedback scores.

But as you can see, you can also achieve perfectly respectable sales with fewer than 10,000 feedback scores. Three of the sellers analyzed have fewer than 10,000 feedback scores, but nevertheless have monthly revenue of more than $500,000. Twelve other sellers have from 10,000 to 50,000 feedback scores and just under 11% of the sellers in this group have over 500,000 feedback scores.

Only 2 sellers within this group have made it into the "millionaire league" of feedback scores and can showcase the silver shooting star on their profiles.

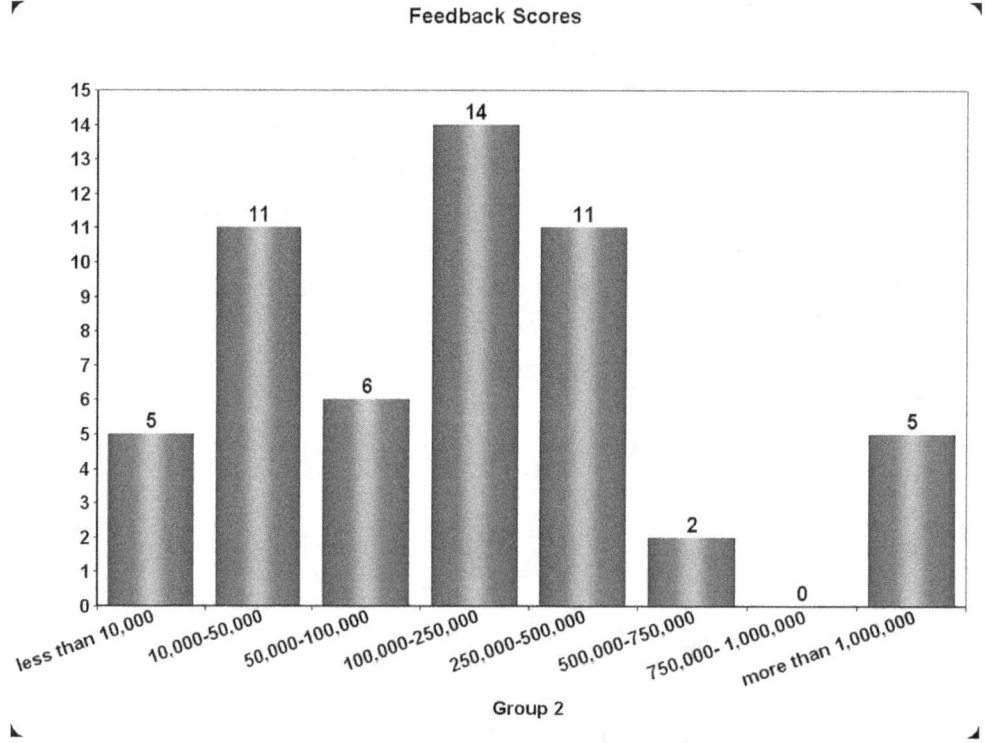

We see a similar result in group 2, the group of sellers who make more than $1 million in sales per month on eBay.

Likewise, five sellers from this group have fewer than 10,000 feedback scores, although they are among the sellers with the highest revenues on eBay.com. Eleven sellers have between 10,000-50,000 feedback scores and the number of sellers that have between 50,000 and 100,000 feedback scores is also relatively high, considering the revenue of six sellers. Overall, nearly 42% of sellers have less than 100,000 feedback scores in this group and make monthly sales of more than $1,000,000.

Five sellers from this group are not only eBay sales millionaires - they make it to the league of feedback millionaires and are the proud carriers of the silver shooting star.

As expected, the scores shift upwards in group 3, the group of sellers who sell more than 30,000 items on eBay.

Here one could almost use the term 'meteor shower', because 25% of the sellers in this group have the coveted silver shooting star.

Nevertheless, the group of sellers who have 100,000-250,000 feedback scores is the largest.

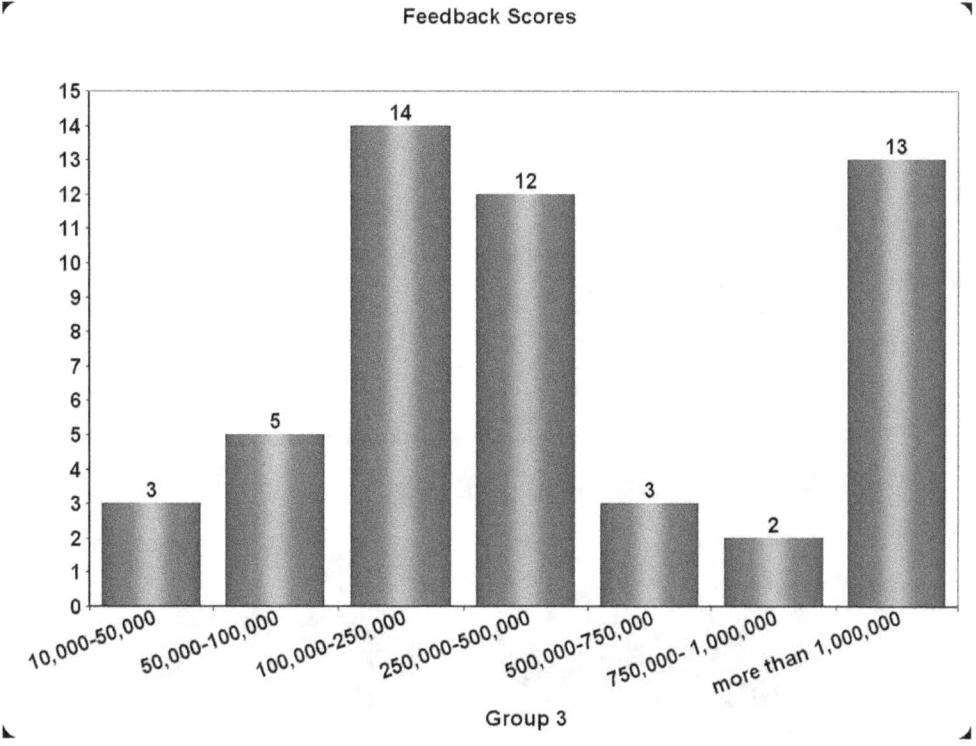

In this group, however, you may also notice that many eBay transactions are not rated, otherwise the numbers would be lower in the range of up to 100,000 feedback scores.

Feedback percentage

On average, the profile rating in group 1 is 99.38% positive, in group 2 the average is 99.2% positve and in group 3 it is 99.05% positive.

Top-rated sellers

How do the various groups compare regarding the award for the top-rated sellers?

Aside from a fast shipment, strict criteria must be met with eBay.com's detailed seller ratings (DSR). As such, only less than 2% of transactions are allowed to receive a detailed seller rating of fewer than three stars under "item as described" and any neutral or negative feedback also plays into the calculation of the seller's status. Sellers who meet the eBay requirements and are awarded a top rating as a seller are rewarded with a discount of 20% on the sales commission, among other things, and they are displayed more prominently in eBay searches.

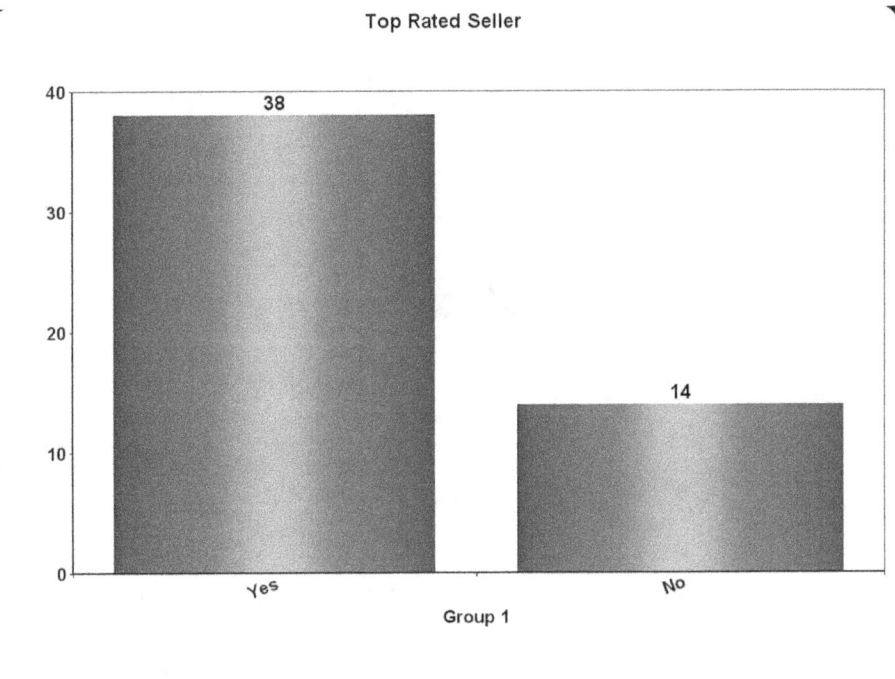

In group 1, i.e. the sellers with sales between $500,000 and $1,000,000, almost 73% of the group belongs to the top-rated sellers; in group 2, the group of sellers that make more than $1 million in sales per month, just under 74% are the top-rated sellers.

The situation looks different in the group of sellers that sell items at low prices in bulk on eBay. Here, fewer than 50% of sellers are top-rated sellers.

These evaluations show that the status of the top-rated seller, which promises better positioning in eBay searches, is not necessarily required to climb the ranks at eBay.com into the league of revenue millionaires or into the league of high-volume sellers.

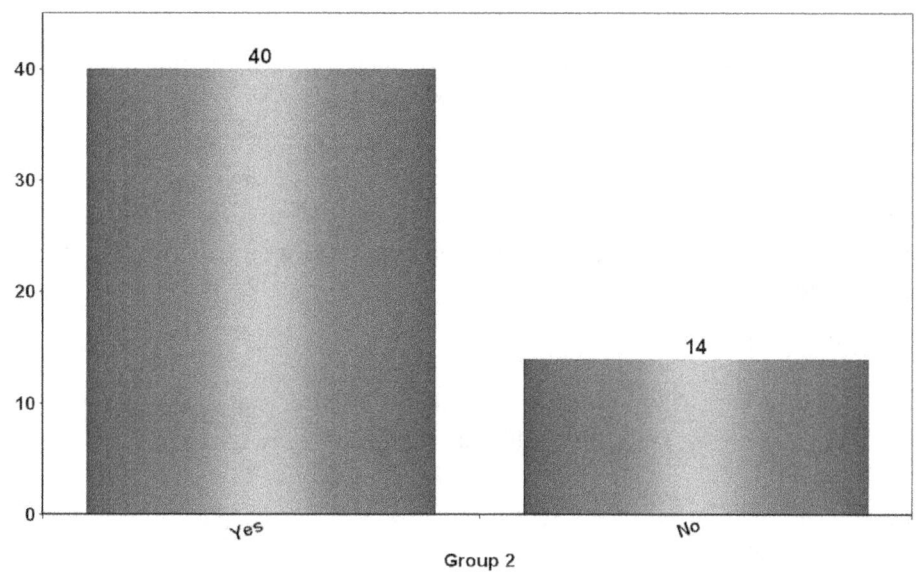

Top Rated Seller

Group 2

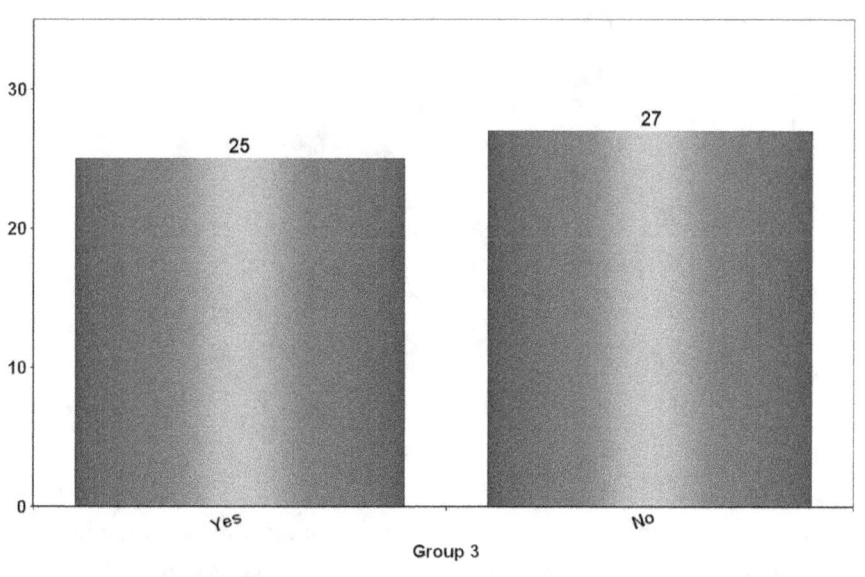

Top Rated Seller

Group 3

Member country

There is a lot of talk about the Chinese "invasion" on eBay, but what do the numbers in the groups say about the sellers that generate high revenue on eBay.com or the ones that sell many items?

In the group of sellers that achieve revenues of between $500,000 and $1 million on eBay, just 11.5% of the sellers are from abroad. There are just six sellers selling from overseas at eBay.com within the 52 sellers analyzed.

One of them sells its products from Japan on eBay.com, another from Britain, three from China and one from Hong Kong.

The entire group of sellers that make more than $1 million in sales at eBay.com is from the USA (100%).

So for these two groups, it's impossible to say that the Chinese are "taking over".

As expected, the group of sellers that sell more than 30,000 items a month looks quite different:

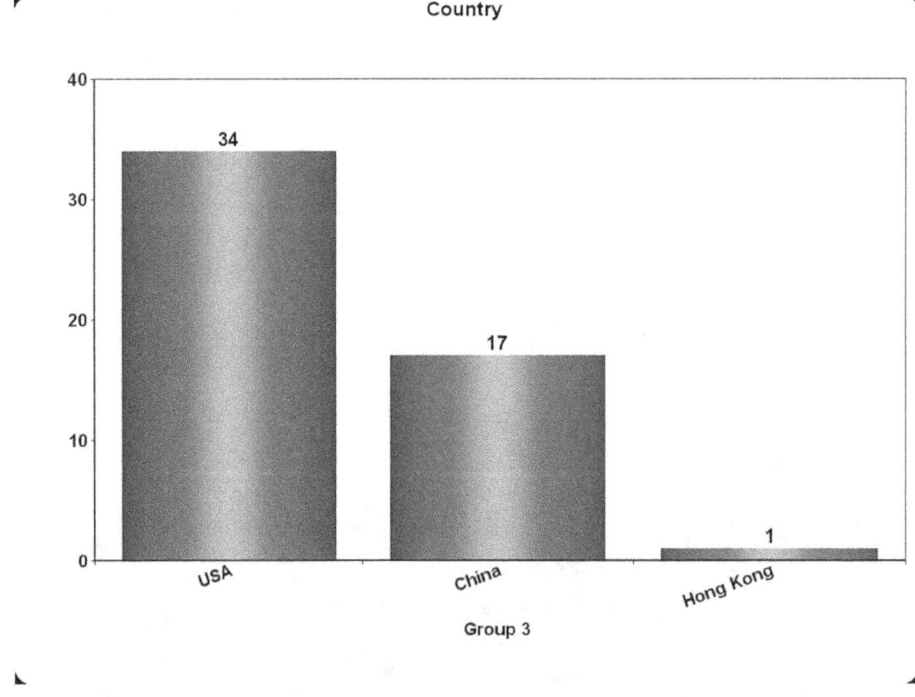

In this group already more than 34% of the sellers are from Asia, and this figure will probably rise before the next evaluation. One should not overlook that in this case on eBay.com, this rather small group has already sold over 2.5 million items a month. That is about 37% more than groups 1 and 2 sell combined. Here, the presence of the Chinese sellers on eBay's marketplace can be seen clearly, also traced by the amount of items sold (often at dumping prices).

Templates

Evaluating the templates amazes me because there is a fairly high potential for optimization.

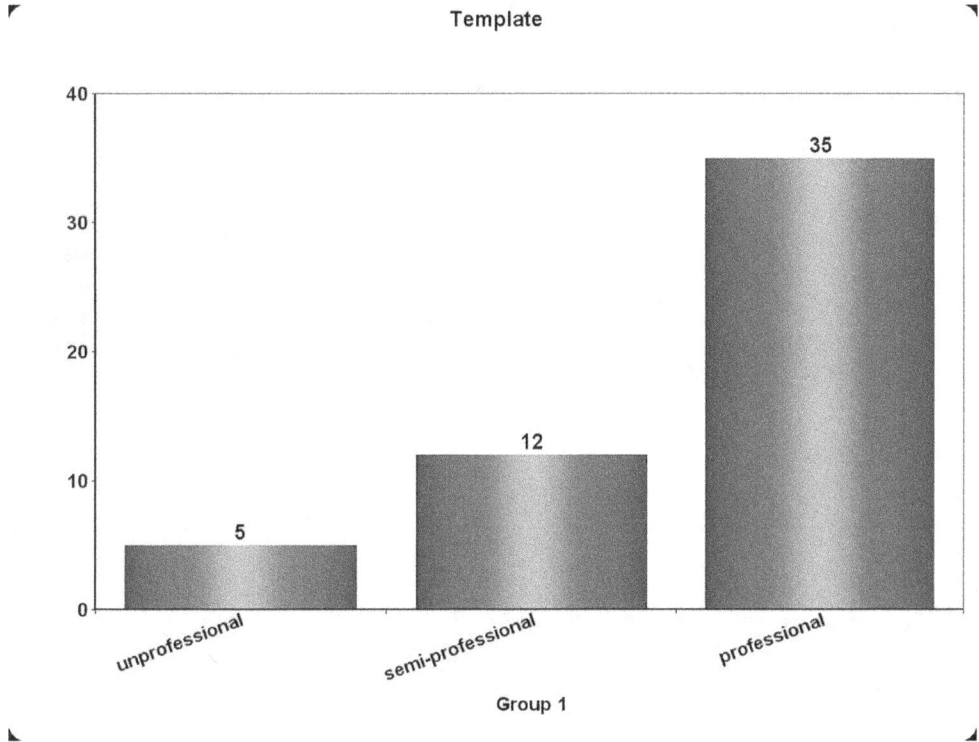

In group 1 "only" 67% of the sellers analyzed have access to a professional template; 33% of the templates in this group are unprofessional or semi-professional.

I don't want to criticize any of the analyzed sellers, but if you look at their listings, you will notice the differences.

Unprofessional templates are templates of the very first eBay generation - templates without images, in different (colored) fonts, templates that have been out of fashion for years.

Semi-professional templates are templates that have no cross-selling or at least, no meaningful cross-selling, and generally use the eBay listing template or similar templates that have been created.

In the second group, things look a little better. Here almost 80% of the sellers have a professional eBay template, but even here there are surprising things to discover. A seller in this group uses pure catalog data almost exclusively and through this tactic, prevents every opportunity for individual differentiation from its competitors.

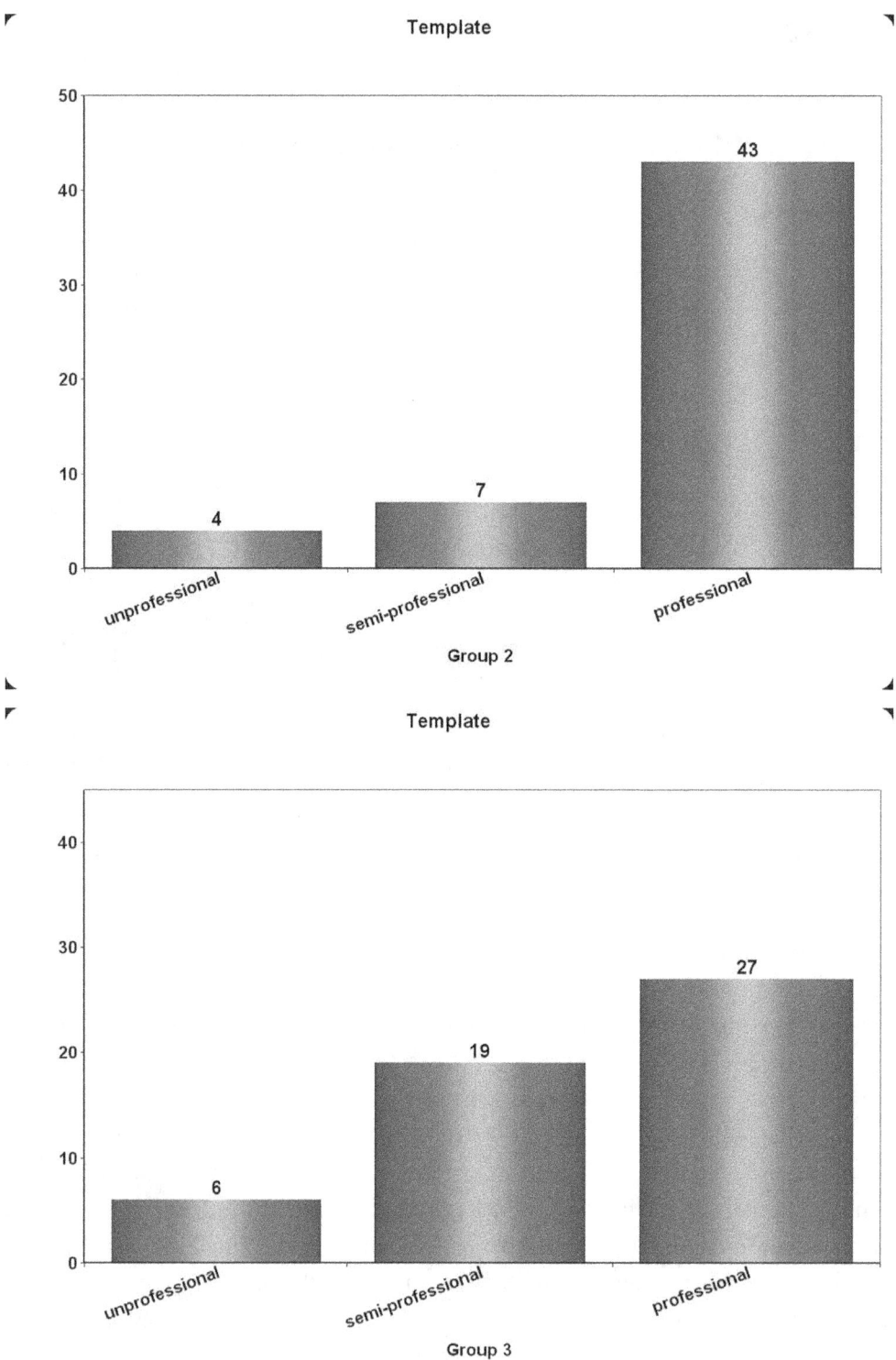

Template

Group 2

Template

Group 3

I was less surprised with group 3, the group of sellers that sell more than 30,000 items on eBay.

Here just under 52% of the sellers have a professional template, but here the revenue gain often comes from the price and supposedly, the template plays no major role for these sellers.

That could be a fatal mistake, in my estimation, because the moment sellers sell items with low profit margins, it becomes important that the buyer purchases more than one item; a good cross-selling would facilitate this.

Looking at all three groups, the following picture emerges (overlap of groups 1 and 2 in group 3 were counted only once:

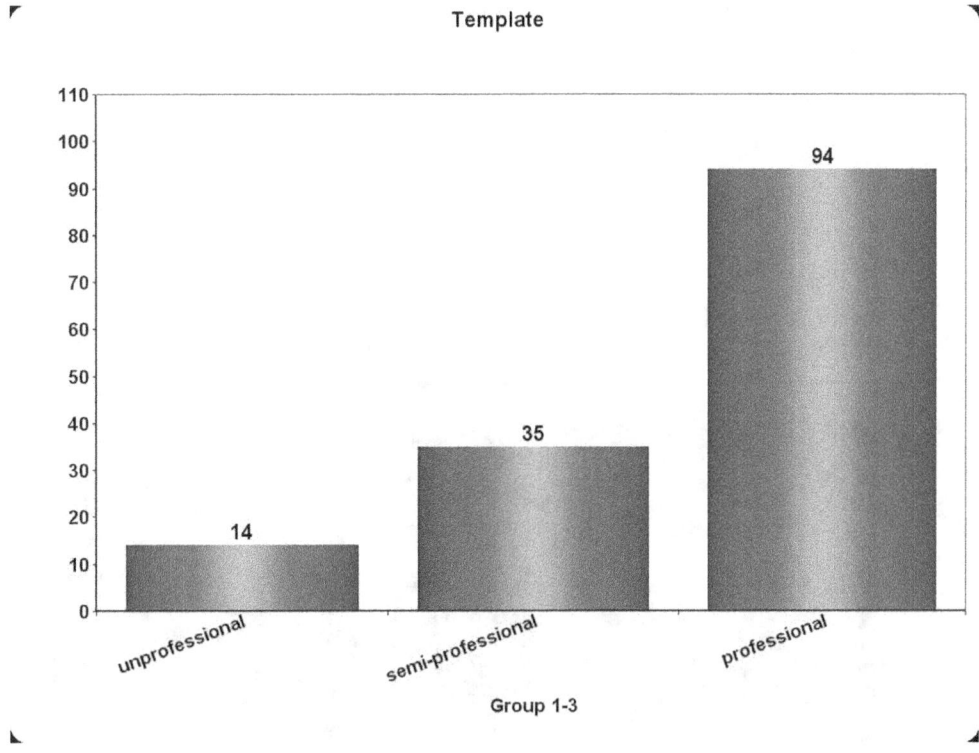

Template

Group 1-3

This chart shows that just under 65% of all sellers have invested in a professional template and the remaining percentage of the sellers could potentially increase its revenues and/or the number of items sold if the sellers would at least implement meaningful cross-selling.

Revenue

Let's take a look at the sales figures.

Our 143 sellers have achieved a total revenue of nearly $163.4 million on eBay.com in the analysis period of 30 days.

Group 1 reached sales of nearly $37.7 million in total, group 2 accounted for total sales of nearly $118 million and group 3 contributed sales of $41.4 million to the overall result. When considering total sales, 15 sellers in group 3 were taken out, accounting for sales of nearly $33.6 million, because they had already been counted in group 1 and 2.

Here you see an overview of the individual groups:

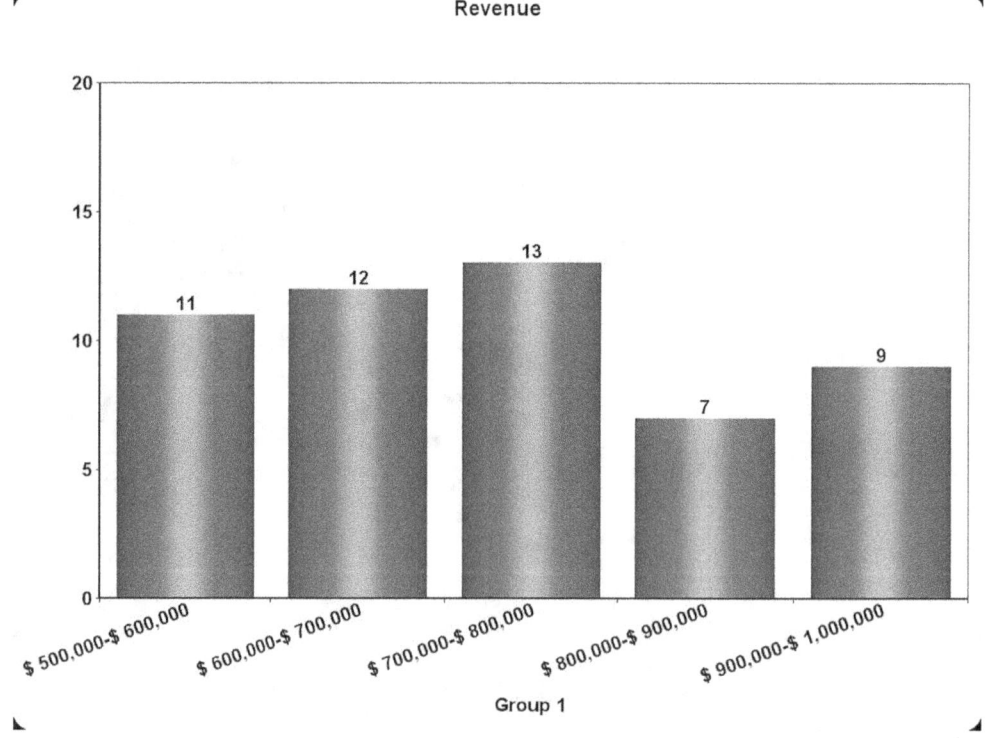

Nearly 17% of the sellers in group 1 are already getting ready to leap into the next dimension and are just about to break through the magic border of more than $1 million in sales per month.

Overall, sales in this group are distributed fairly equally.

Revenue

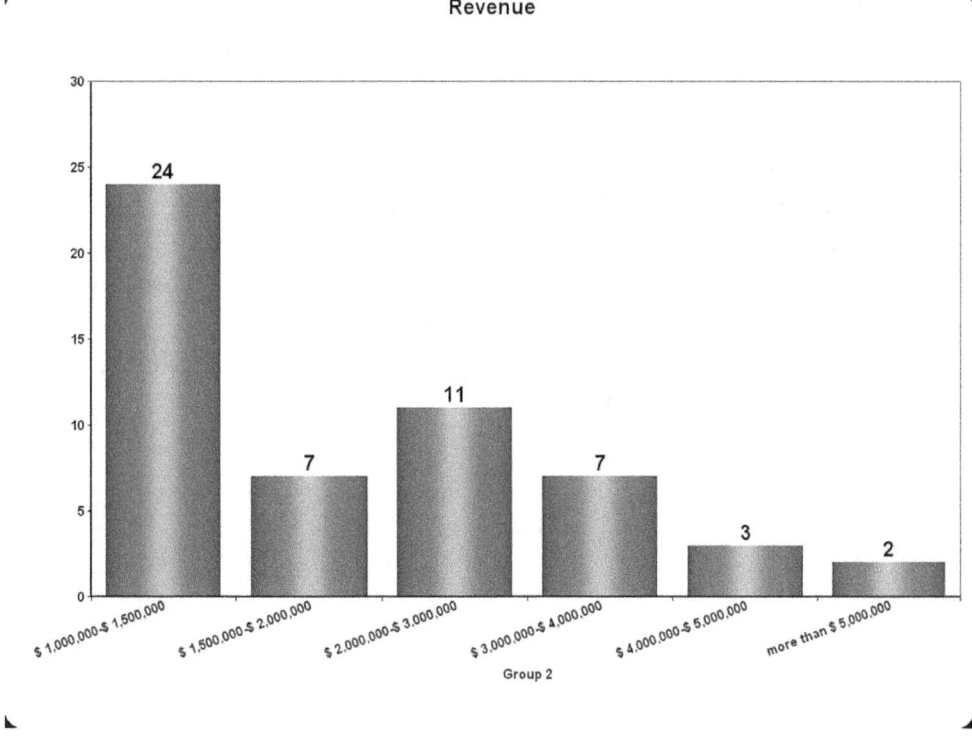

Revenue

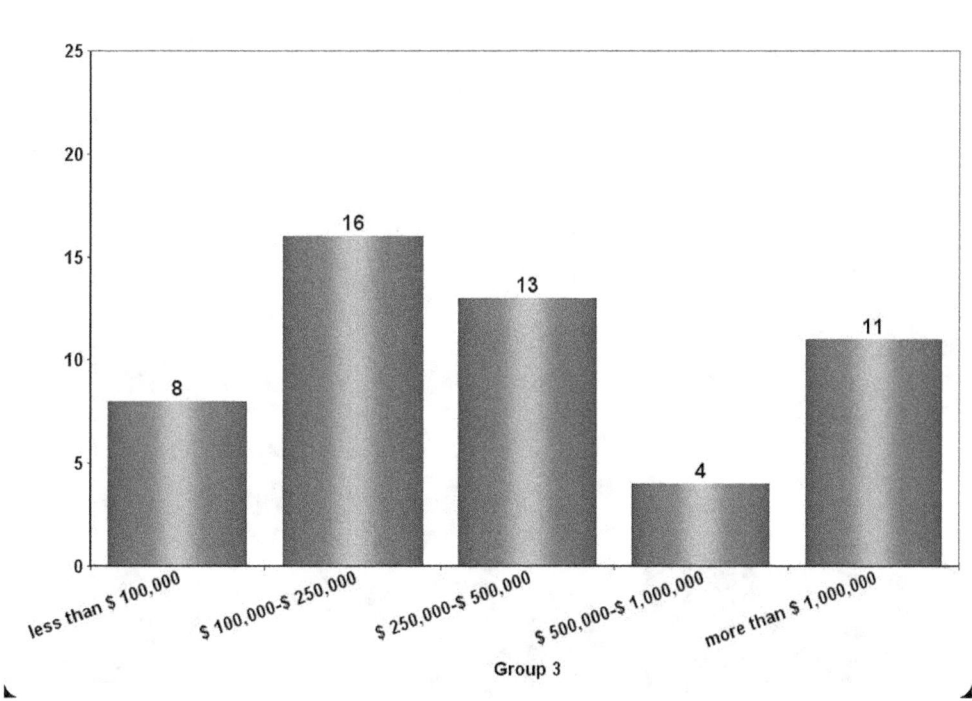

The second group's sales could be especially astonishing for those who have long since written off eBay, because more than 60% of the sellers in this group not only generate more than $1 million in sales per month on eBay.com, but sales hit more than $2,000,000. The two top sellers in this group are the eBay sellers "bluetek" and "altatac", both of which have generated sales of more than $6,000,000 a month, respectively, in the analyzed time period.

Since both sellers sell more than 30,000 items per month, they are also represented in group 3.

What does it look like overall in the group of sellers who sell the most on eBay.com?

Eight of the sellers in the group of high-volume sellers sold more than 30,000 products and through them, generated less than $100,000 in sales per month.

Eleven still belong in group 2 because they not only sell lots of products, but they also earn a respectable revenue of more than $1,000,000.

Average selling price

In connection with revenue, the average selling prices are also interesting.

In group 1, the average selling price per item is $212.75. In group 2 the average selling price is $3,247.63, but here four sellers heavily skew the average with exceptionally high average selling prices between $8,658 and $122,970.

Leaving these four "exceptional sellers" out, the average selling price of this group is $235.90, putting it near group 1.

In group 3 the average sales price is only $16.69.

Overall, the average selling price in group 1 is under $100, accounting for 57% of the sellers.

30% are still in the range between $100 and $500, with the air getting thin for this group. Only 11% of this group has an average selling price of over $1,000.

In this group, the lowest average price is $5.24; the highest average price is $2,053.

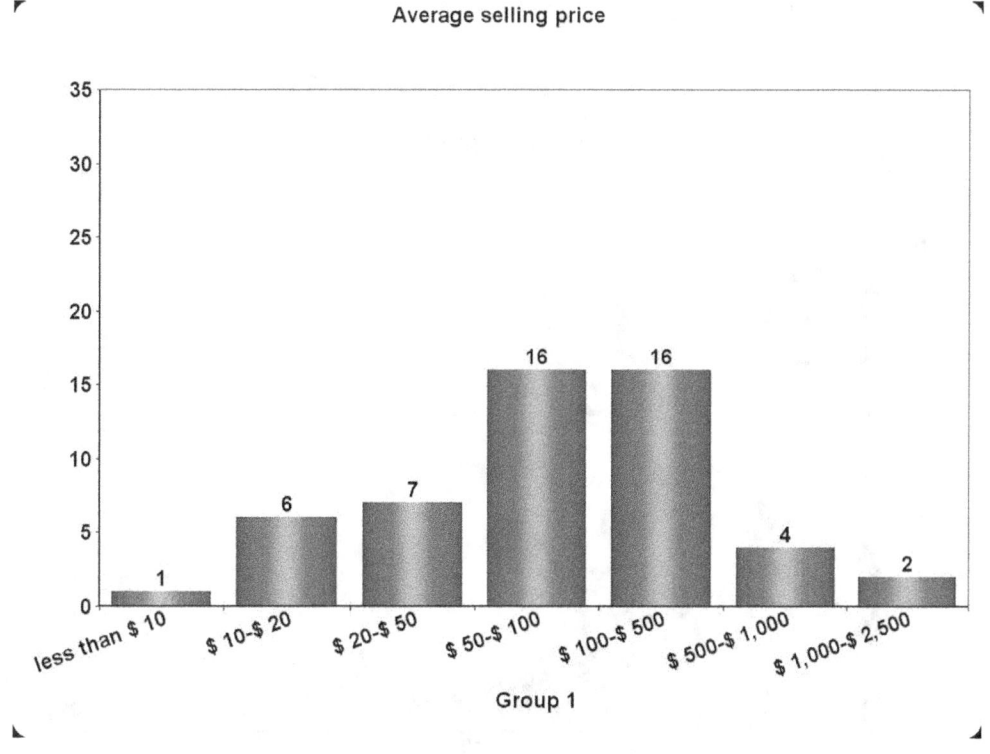

Average selling price

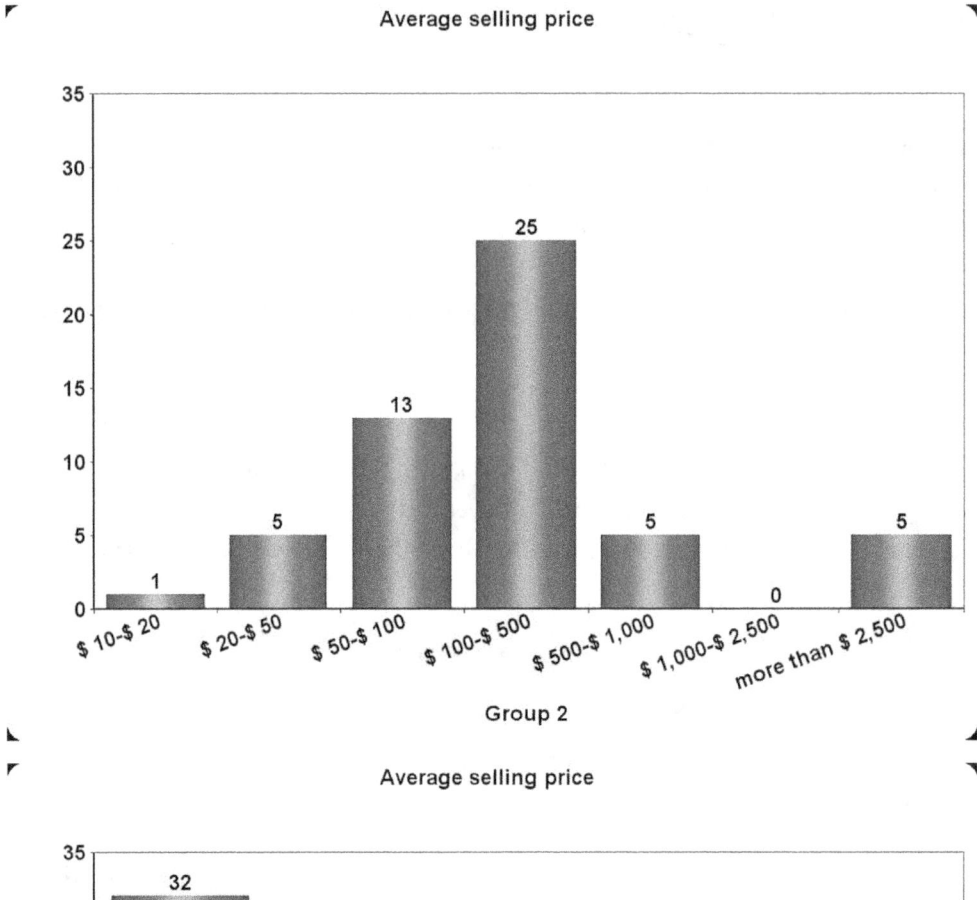

Group 2

Average selling price

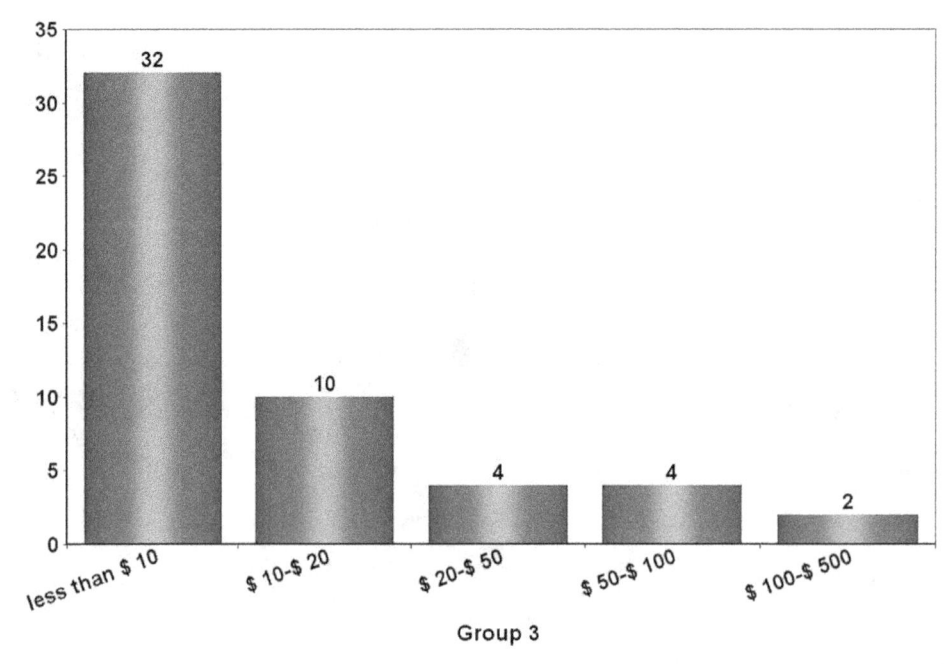

Group 3

The second group shows a similar picture, although this group generated more than $1 million a month.

The largest range is the range between $100 and $500, where almost 46% of the sellers in this group fall.

But even here only less than 10% reach an average selling price of more than $1,000.

The seller with the lowest average price is $22.15; the seller with the highest average price falls at $122,970.

In group 3 the situation almost looks terrifying.

With over 30,000 items sold per month, the average retail price for just under 61% of the sellers is under $10.

From that, sellers must pay for eBay and PayPal fees, merchandise and shipping material and often even the shipping costs as well as the employees, because a one-man show cannot send out the daily minimum of 1,000 items.

The lowest average price in this group is $0.76 - an average price, which cannot work out - the highest price is $137.22.

Considering the figures it is not surprising that the presence of Chinese sellers is quite strong in this group.

Total number of listed items

In the total number of listed items of the three groups it's clear how dominant these three groups are on the eBay.com marketplace.

The total number of listed items means that when a seller creates a listing on eBay with ten items available for purchase, for example, the total number would be ten, even if the seller only listed one listing.

In total, these 143 sellers (15 are subtracted from group 3, because they were already counted in groups 1 and 2) listed an incredible number of 446,117,842 items on eBay.com.

47% of these items are attributable to group 3; group 2 represents almost 31%, and last but not least is group 1 with just under 22%.

Here is the detailed analysis of group 1:

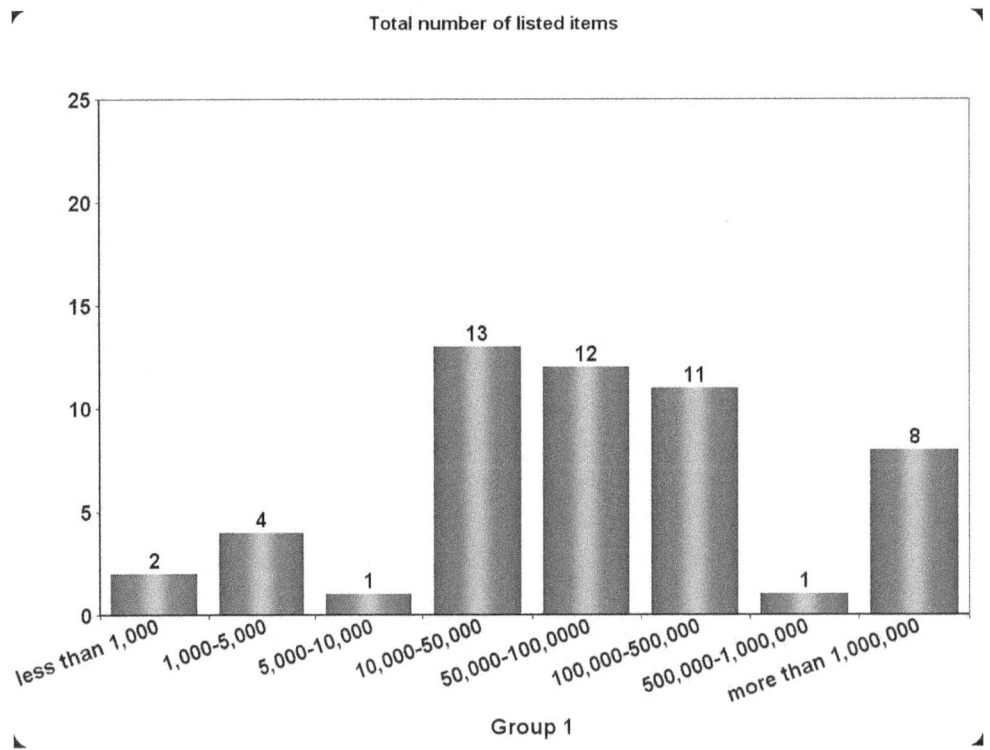

Total number of listed items

Group 1

Only two sellers of group 1 have a total of less than 1,000 listings for sale on eBay.com, while at the other end of the scale there are eight sellers listing more than 1,000,000 listings for sale on eBay.com.

On average, each seller of this group lists some 1.8 million listings on eBay.com. The range here is enormous and ranges from 780 listings to 53 million listings.

In group 2, a similar picture can be seen, although the middle section is somewhat more balanced.

Here the average is 2.6 million listings; the enormous spread lies between nearly 170 and 90 million listings.

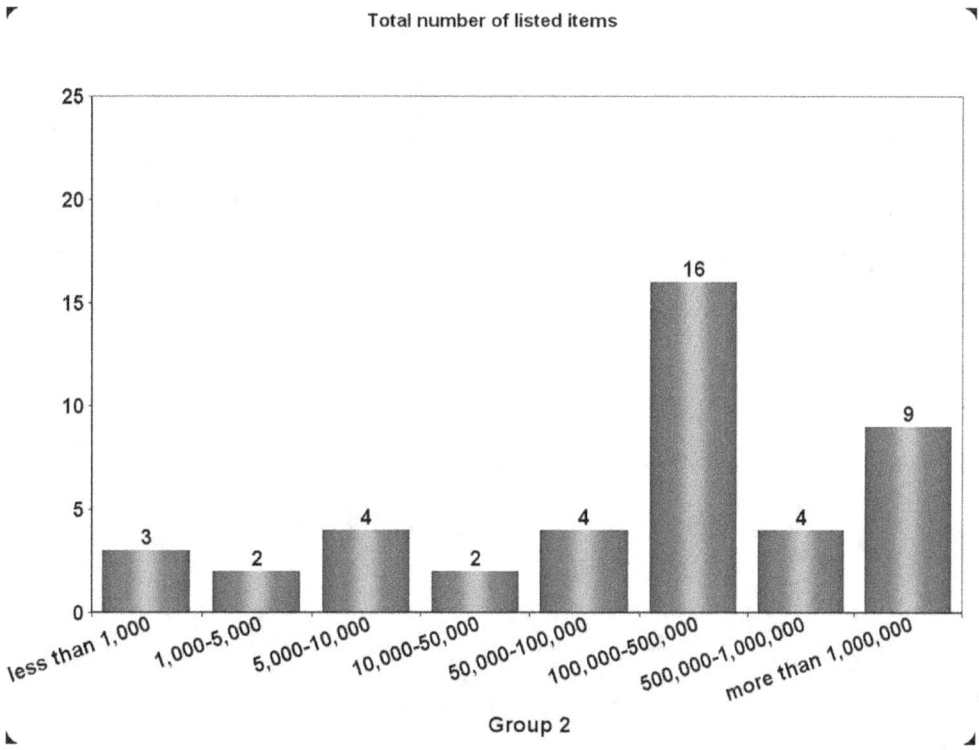

Total number of listed items

Group 2

As expected, the group 3 leads this area with 16 sellers who list more than one million items for sale on eBay.com. This represents about 30% of the sellers in this group.

On average, each seller of this group lists four million items, but here, too, there is a large range of between 32,000 and 90 million items listed.

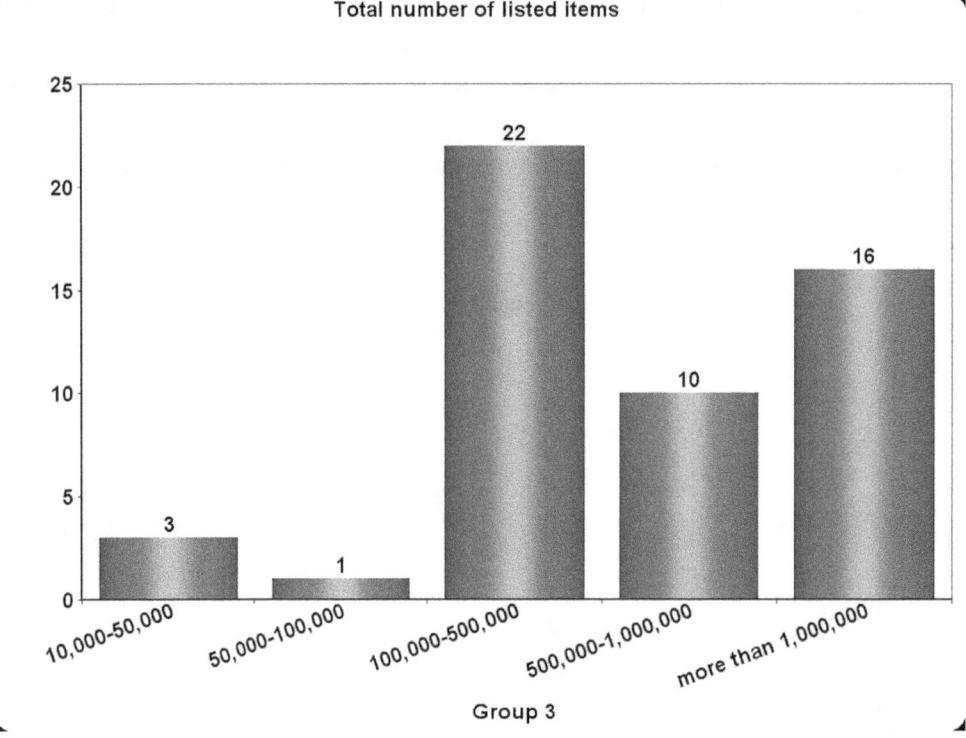

Total number of listed items

Group 3

Items listed

Now let's take a look at the number of items listed.

If we stick with the example above, a seller has listed an item for which ten units are for sale within the listing, then there is a total number of ten listed items - for the listed items that we're now looking at, only the listing itself counts - regardless of the number of items available within this range - in this case there would be one listing.

Let's consider only the items listed, then we see the figures above more in perspective (total numbers of the listed items), still, more than five million listings are left listed by this fairly small number of only 143 sellers on eBay.com.

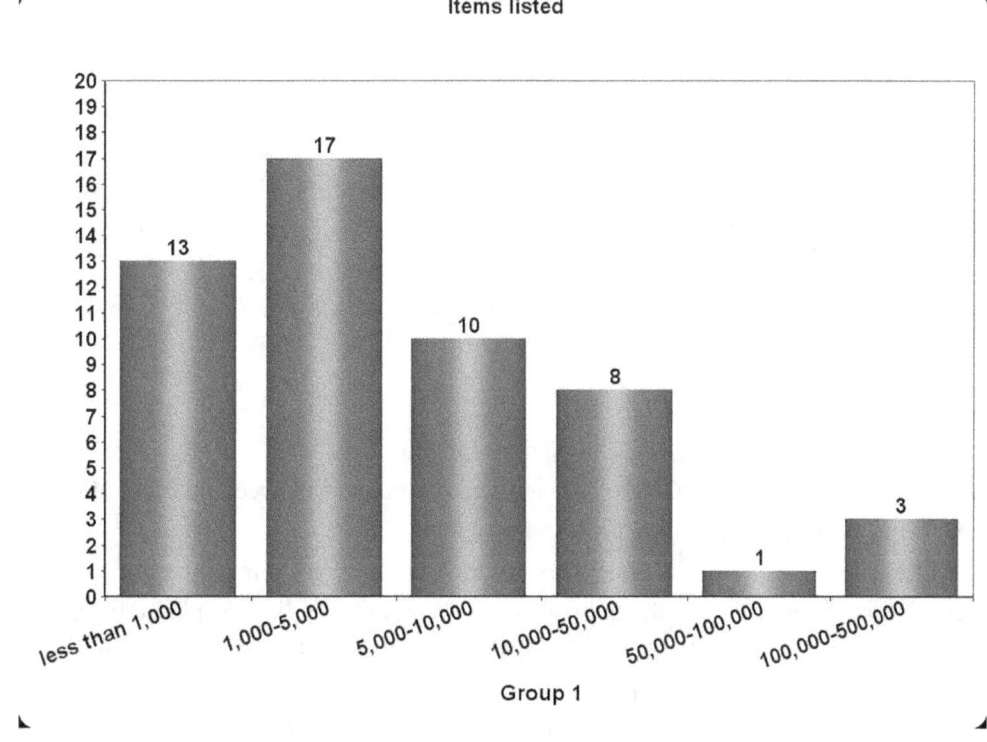

Overall, the margin for the sellers in group 1 is enormous.

The seller that listed the fewest items in this group has just 62 items listed; the seller with the highest number of items listed in this group has 409,600 items listed.

On average, the sellers from this group have listed almost 22,000 items.
Nearly 58% of the sellers have listed fewer than 5,000 listings.

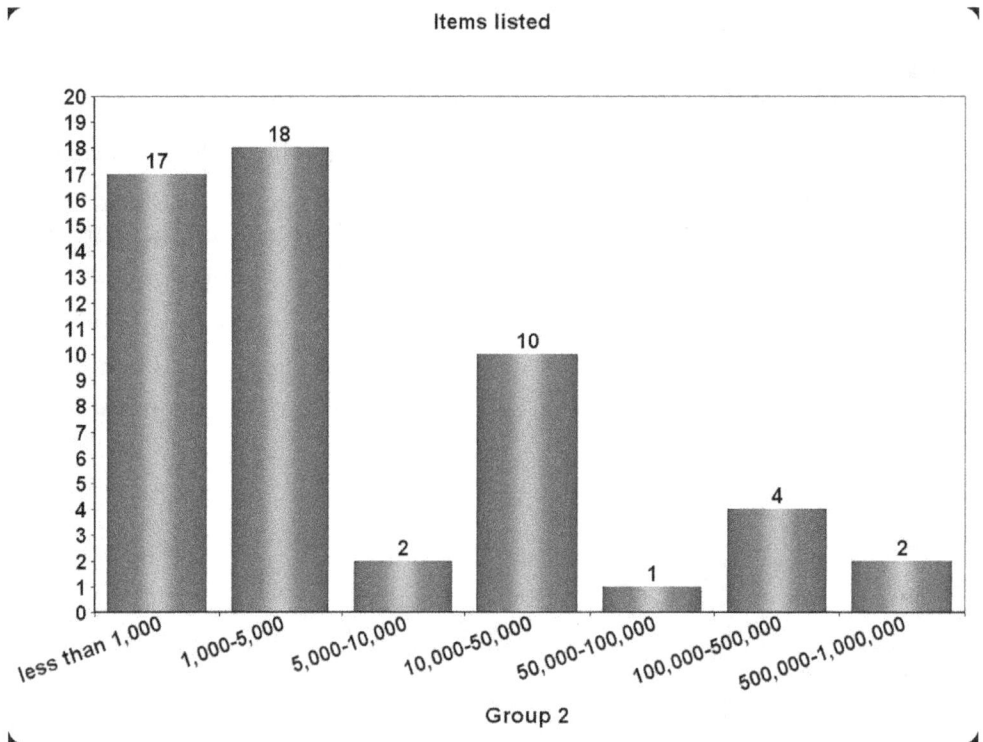

In the second group we see a similar picture.

64% of the sellers have listed up to 5,000 listings on eBay.com.

The average is just under 43,000 listed listings, and the range is between an incredible 19 listings extending up to 660,000 listings.

In the third group, the end of the scale does not look different from in groups 1 and 2. Only two sellers have listed more than 500,000 listings, yet the number of listings placed by sellers of this group range between 100,000 and 500,000 listings, more than that of the sellers in the other two groups.

On average, the sellers of this group have listed almost 73,500 listings - more than the groups 1 and 2 combined.

Again, there are of course enormous outliers on both ends - at the lower end we find a seller who has listed only 60 items, while the seller at the top has just under 665,000 listed items.

Items listed

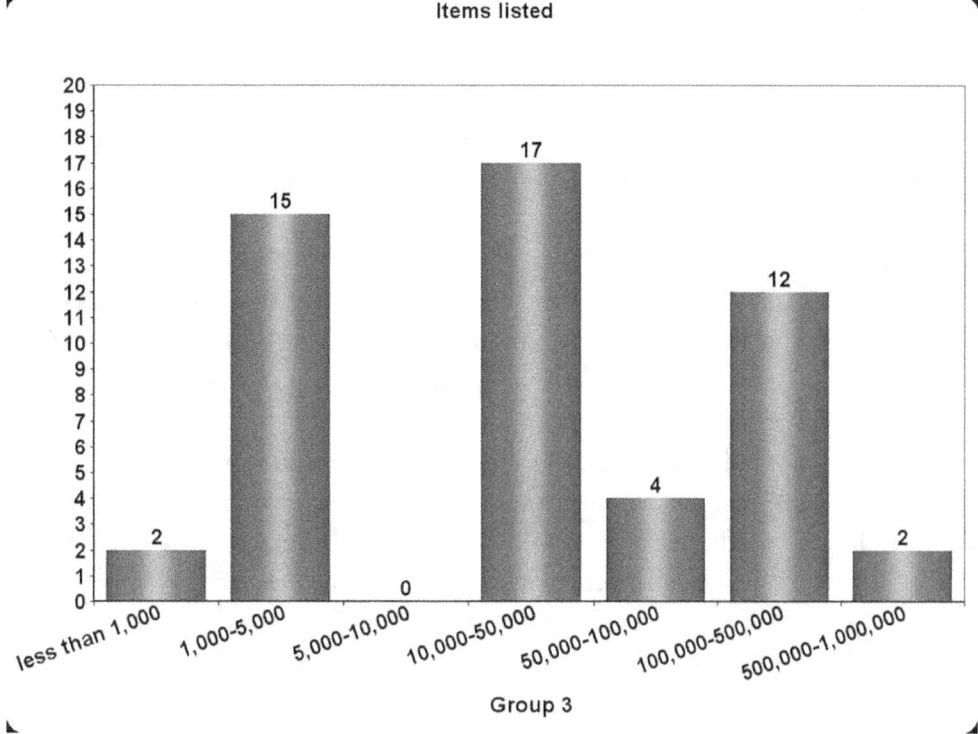

Group 3

Successful listings

Considering the number of listed listings begs the question, how many of the listings were successful and how many items have the sellers of these listings sold?

Let's start with the successful listings:

A total of nearly 1.4 million listings of the three groups were successful.

Of this amount, 270,000 listings went to the first group, followed by group 2 with nearly 400,000 successful listings and group 3 represents nearly one million of the total successful listings. (In the calculation of the total, 15 sellers were subtracted from group 3 again, as they were already represented in groups 1 and 2.)

In group 1, an average of just under 5,200 listings were successful, in which case a seller with almost 88,000 successful listings skewed the result. Leaving this seller out, an average of nearly 3,500 successful listings is reflected in the graph. Nearly 67% of sellers lie in the range of up to 5,000 successful listings, only one manages to make it over the 50,000 mark.

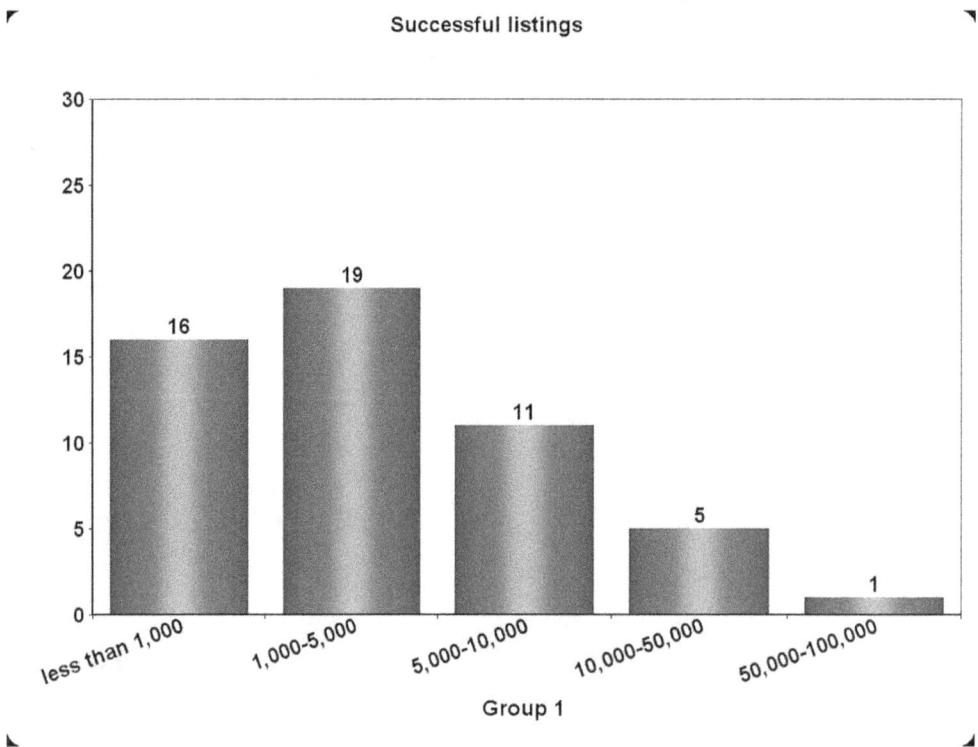

In group 2, we see a similar picture. Here 71% of the sellers are in the range of up to 5,000 successful listings, but one seller makes it over the boundary of more than 100,000 successful listings.

On average, nearly 7,400 successful listings were recorded by sellers from group 2, but again, one seller is the outlier with 116,000 successful listings. On the other hand, there is a seller who only recorded 19 successful listings, and another who claims only 34; this is the explanation for the numbers on the graph in which the majority of sellers can be found, the range of up to 5,000 successful listings.

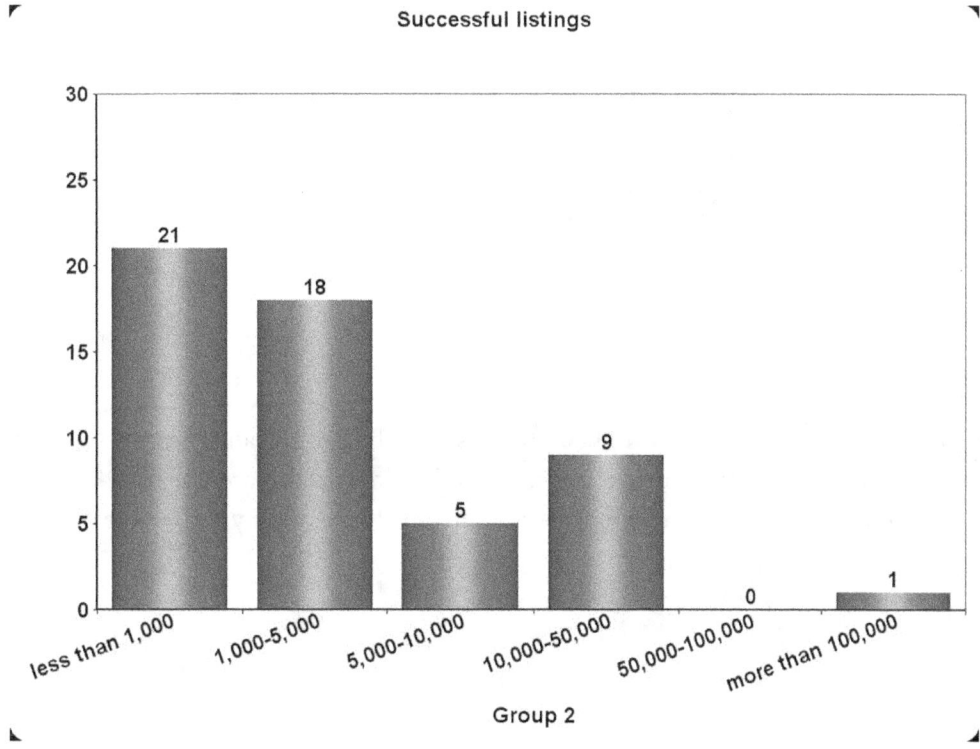

In group 3, the average would be just under 20,000 items sold, but, as in groups 1 and 2, the range is so vast that one can hardly discern a meaningful average.

The seller with the fewest successful listings has only 60 successful listings (out of which, however, he sold 37,500 items); the seller at the other end of the scale had 116,000 successful listings.

In the graph, the result is as follows:

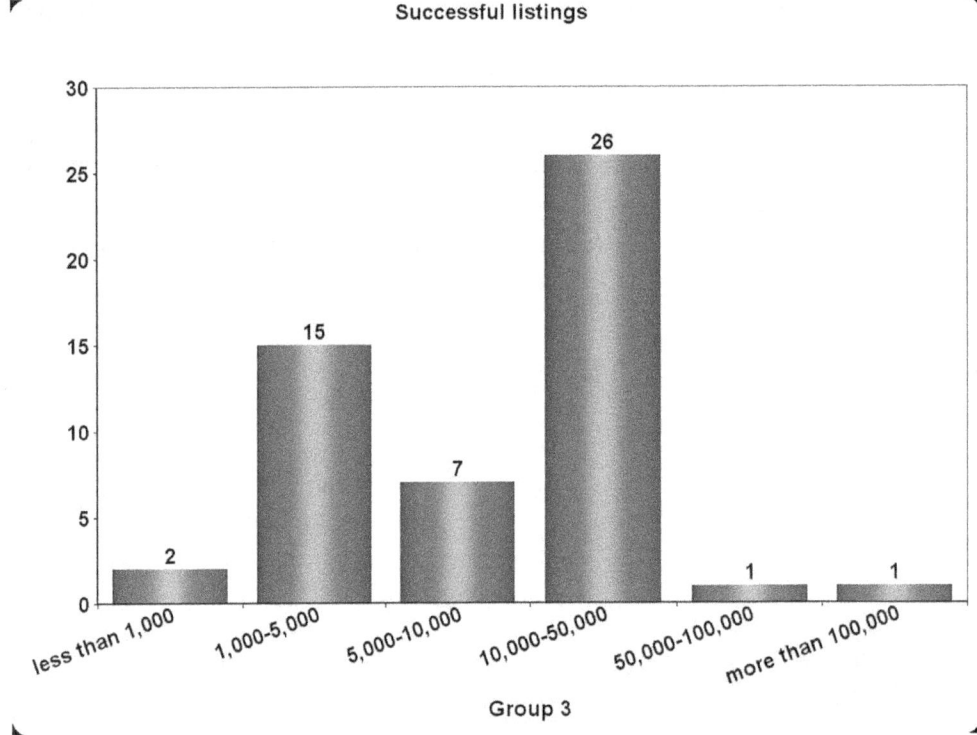

Half the sellers are in the range of 10,000-50,000 successful listings, and the only significant exception is in the range from 1,000 to 5,000 successful listings. In this area, nearly 28% of the sellers qualify for this group. The remainder is distributed almost equally among the other areas.

Items sold

The next interesting question: How many items have our 143 sellers sold in total on eBay.com?

Here, we must make a distinction - successful listings are listings from which at least one item has been sold. A seller has created a listing on eBay, from which 10 items are listed, and if two products are sold from this listing then the seller has created a successful listing, but in the number of items sold, two are counted.

In total, our 143 sellers sold almost 3.5 million items on eBay.com in just one month.

Group 1 represents 750,000 of the products sold, group 2 accounts for nearly 1.1 million items sold to the overall result, and group 3, the largest group, accounts for just under 2.5 million items sold. (Again, 15 sellers who overlap in the groups were counted only once in the overall results.)

In group 1, the mid range is 1,000-25,000 items sold. 80% of the sellers in this group fall in these three areas, with the range from 10,000 to 25,000 items sold being the most represented.

At the bottom of the range we find a seller who has sold 486 items; at the top, a seller with nearly 102,000 items sold.

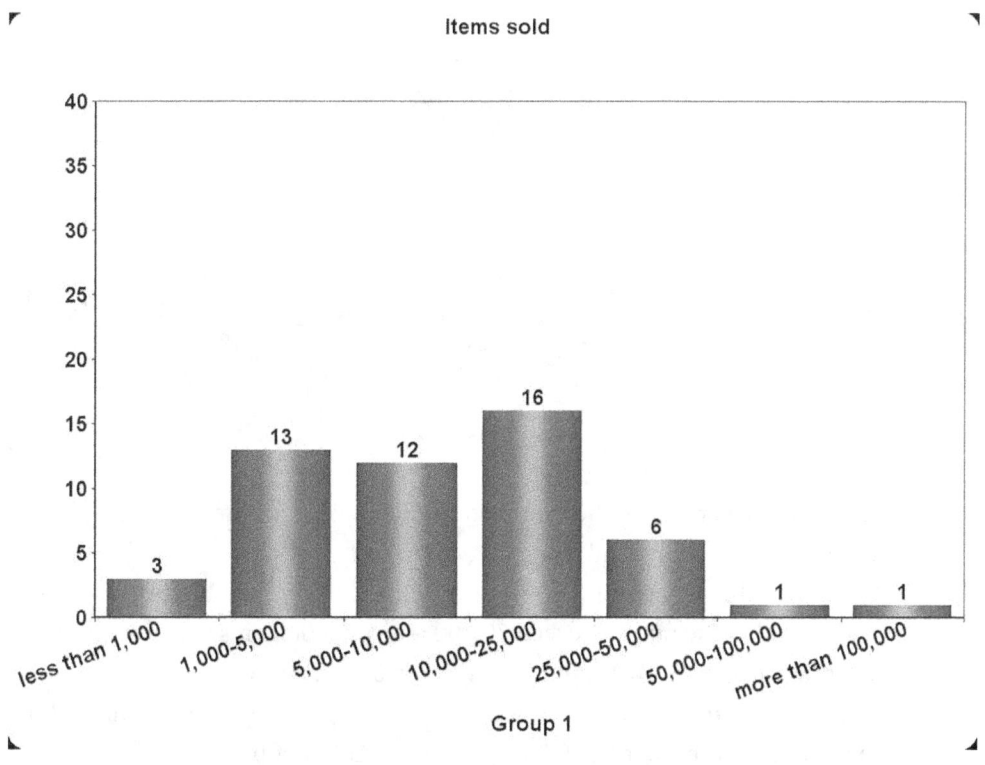

Items sold

Group 1

In group 2, the mid range moves slightly lower.

The three strongest areas are the combined ranges from 5,000 to 50,000 items sold. Again, almost 80% of the sellers fall in this triad, which is different from group 1 in its low and high points, however.

However, the highest range we have in this group is between 10,000-25,000 items sold.

In this group, the range again is huge. At the beginning of the scale are two sellers with negligible numbers of 34 and 77 items sold each, from which they generate monthly revenue of more than $1 million. At the other end of the scale there is a seller who has sold close to 116,000 items.

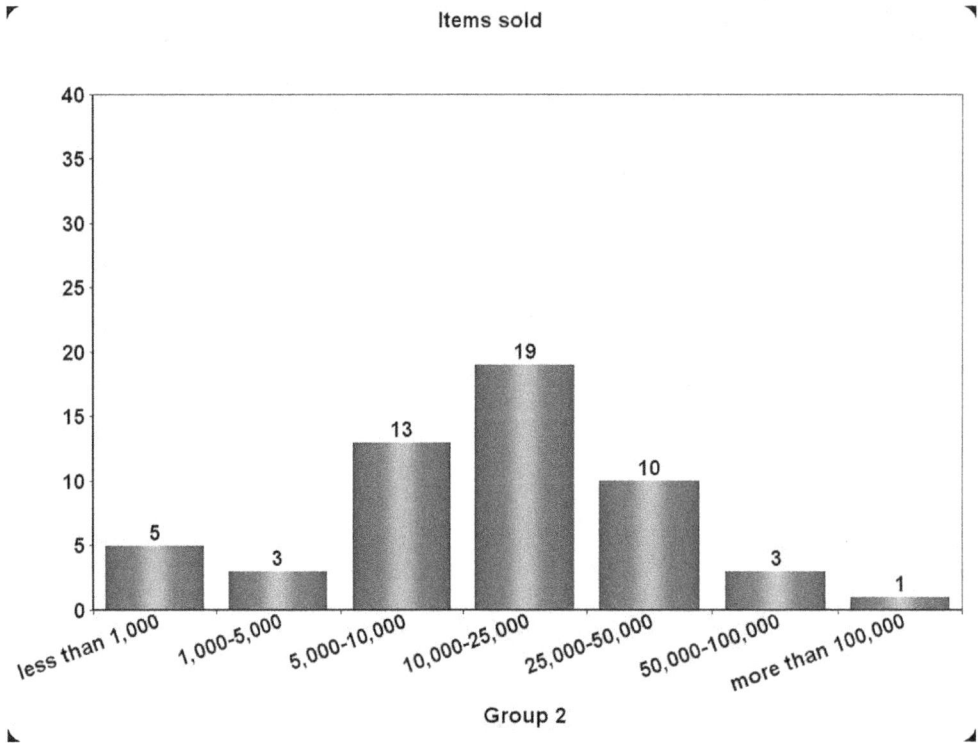

Group 2

In group 3, 75% of the sellers are in the range from 25,000 to 50,000 items sold. It's clear that here, the range of up to 30,000 items sold is missing completely.

But even in this group, the sales become fewer and farther between the higher we go. Yes, ten sellers from this group fall in the range between 50,000 and 100,000 items sold each month, but in this group we only find three sellers with more than 100,000 items sold.

In this group, the range is not quite as dramatic as in the other two groups because all of the sellers fall into the category of more than 30,000 items sold. At the upper limit there is one seller with 116,000 items sold, which already leads group 2. This seller is followed by another with 110,000 items sold, which is found only in group 3.

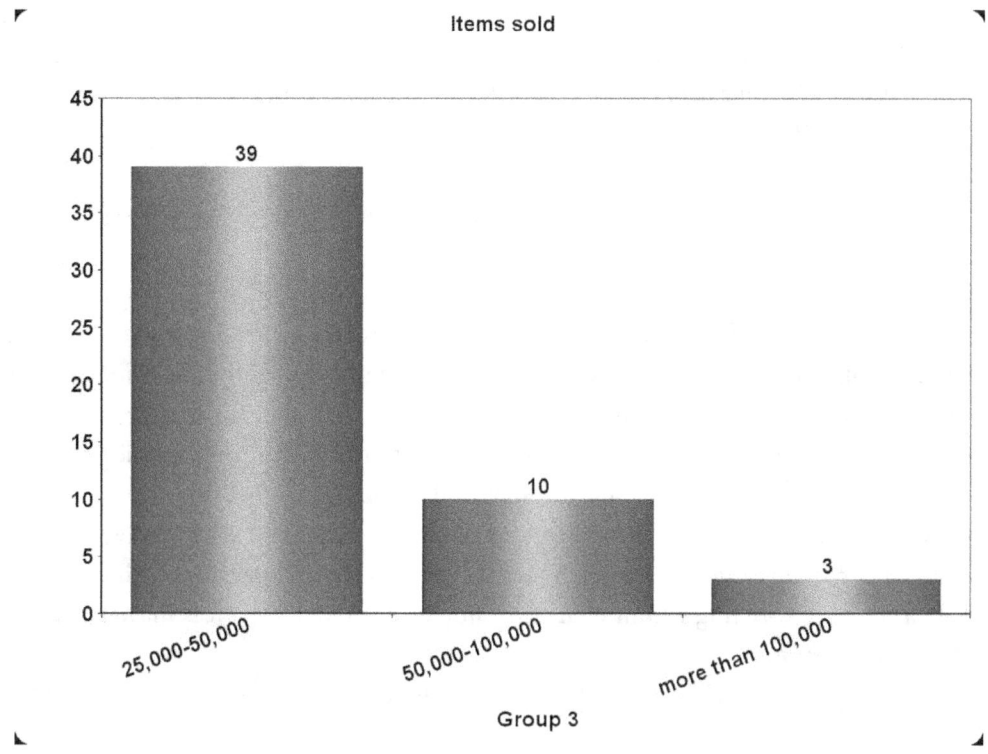

Sell-through rate

In the competitive analysis it's often very revealing to take a look at the sales rate of the competitor. Do the competitors know the marketplace well, or are they trying to fish in stormy seas? In general, competitors with an extremely poor sell-through rate are much more easily overtaken than competitors that dominate their market.

How is the sell-through rate calculated?

Let's continue with the example with a listing where you sell ten items and we continue to assume that you have ten such listings online on eBay.

You would then have ten offers with ten units, i.e. 100 offers on eBay.

If you now sell five items from five of your listings, you have sold 25 items, however, the sale rate is 50% since only half of your listings were successful, while in the other half no items were sold. There is either no demand or your competitors are undercutting your price, or they are better positioned than you are on eBay. There may be many reasons for this, but the better a seller knows the marketplace, the higher the sell-through rate usually is.

There are, of course, reasons for listing items on eBay every once in a while, where it's clear that the chances for a sale are quite low. Such reasons could be to draw visitors with high-demand keywords to a good cross-selling within your own shop or even to leave traces in categories that you don't primarily serve.

Here a seller might have higher prices than those of its competitors and for that reason the seller will sell less, but in doing this, the goal is not primarily the successful sale. Overall, these measures should be avoided because they don't reduce the sales quota to the extent that it slips into the area of concern. On the other hand, sellers who choose to start with extremely low priced items in auction format, often have an extremely high sell-through rate, although they have to sell some items well below value.

You must also bear this in mind when you look at the sell-through rate. In group 1, the sell-through rate is below 50% for 22% of the sellers - an almost alarming value that indicates a need for improvement.

After all, the sell-through rate is over 75% for almost 58% of sellers.

The lowest sell-through rate is just 2.61%.

For one seller who has a sell-through rate of 3.24%, you can clearly see that the sell-through rate reflects its entire presence on eBay.com.

The template is unprofessional and the seller runs a shop without a recognizable profile.

In the total number of items the seller has over twelve million items in over 208,000 listings listed and "only" sold nearly 6,700.

Sell-through rate

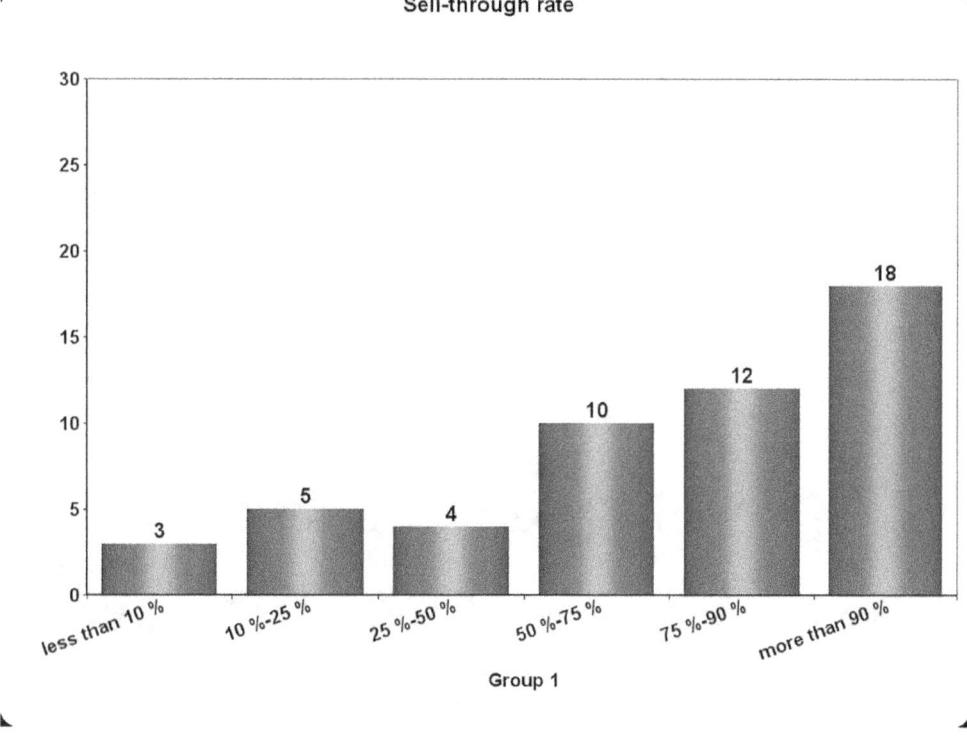

Group 1

Sell-through rate

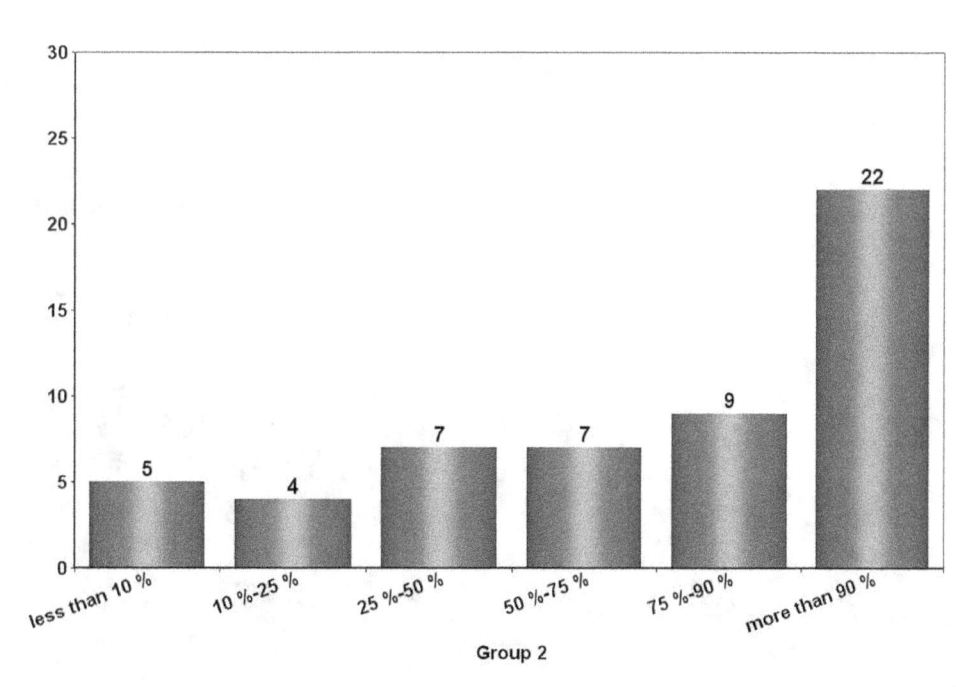

Group 2

Sell-through rate

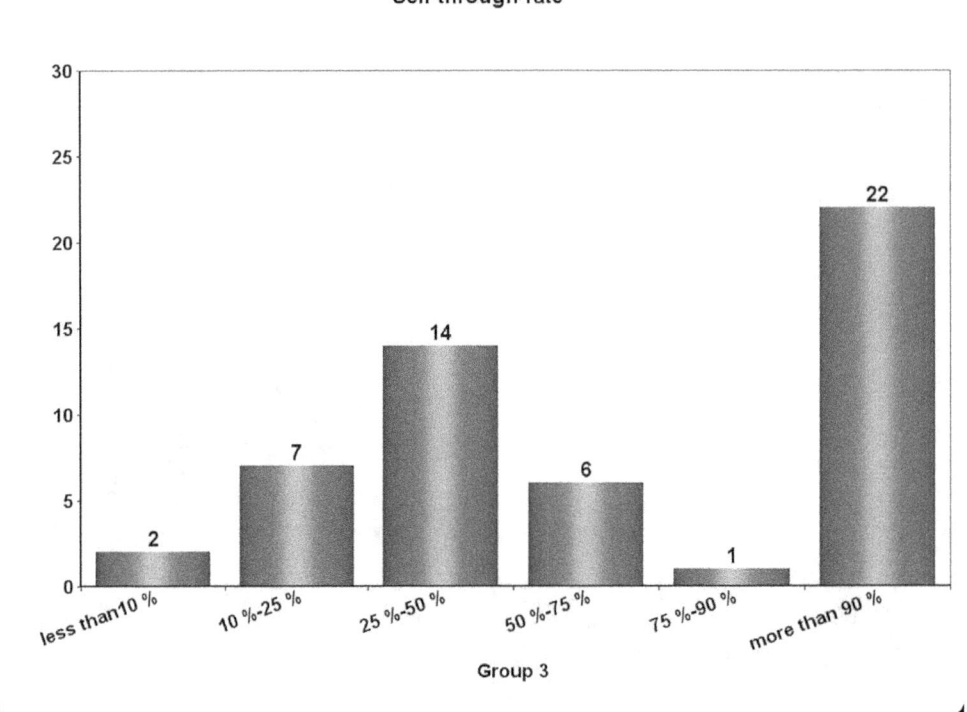

Group 3

Sell-through rate

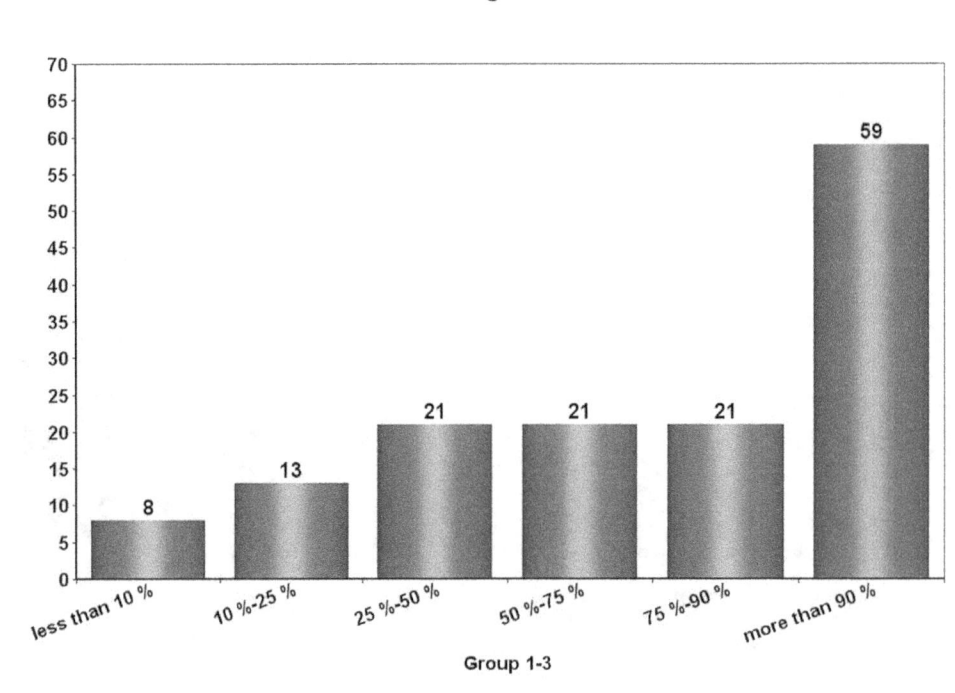

Group 1-3

Here, a little more knowledge of the marketplace would certainly be good and could improve the results.

In group 2, it is no better:

Here nearly 30% of the sellers are below 50%; on the other side of the scale, there are 58% who have a sell-through rate of more than 75%.

The lowest rate in this group is 3.85%.

In group 3 we see a similar picture: almost 45% of the sellers are below 50%, almost 45% above 75%. The lowest sell-through rate was 3.85%.

Overall, this results in the following picture:

36% of the sellers analyzed are selling at a rate of less than 50%; almost 15% of them are below 25%, 56% are above 75%.

Selling format

As already mentioned, the way an item is sold plays a role in the sell-through rate and therefore we'll now take a look at the listing formats:

In group 1, 48% of the sellers rely solely on the fixed price or shop format, which means, on the other hand, that nearly 52% of the sellers post their listings to some extent in the auction format on eBay. 33% of the sellers in group 1 list more than 50% of their listings in auction format.

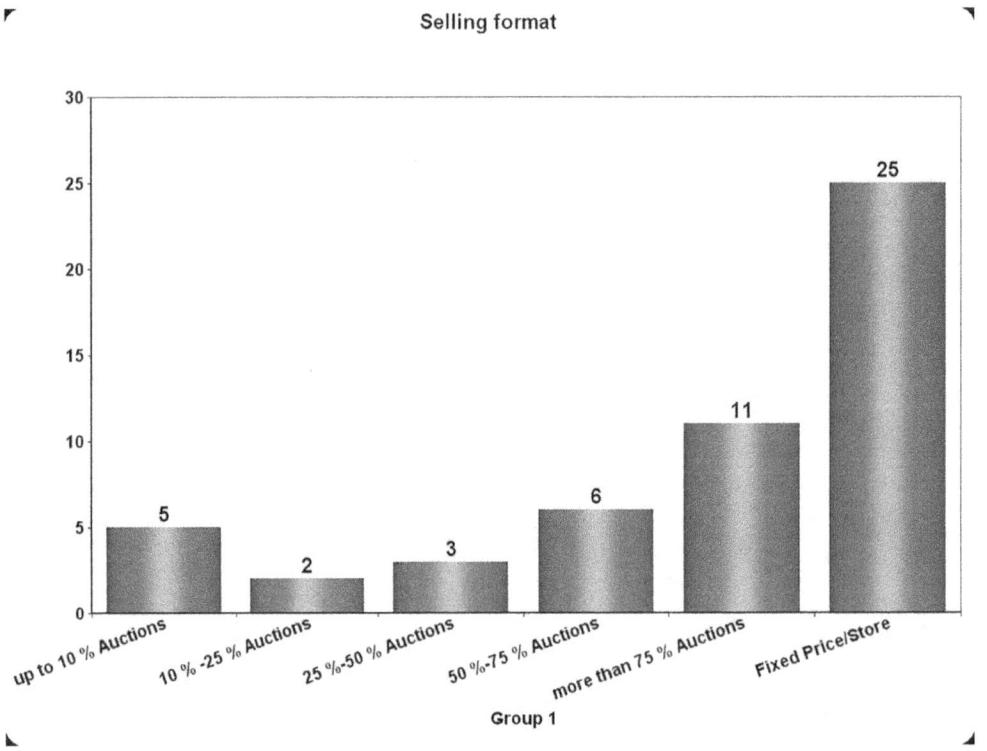

In group 2, the numbers are similar: nearly 52% of the sellers rely solely on the fixed price or shop listing, 48% also use auctions, 33% of the sellers list even more than 50% in auctions.

In group 3, just under 35% of sellers make their listings exclusively in fixed price or shop listing format, 65% also list on auction, 46% list more than 50% in the auction format.

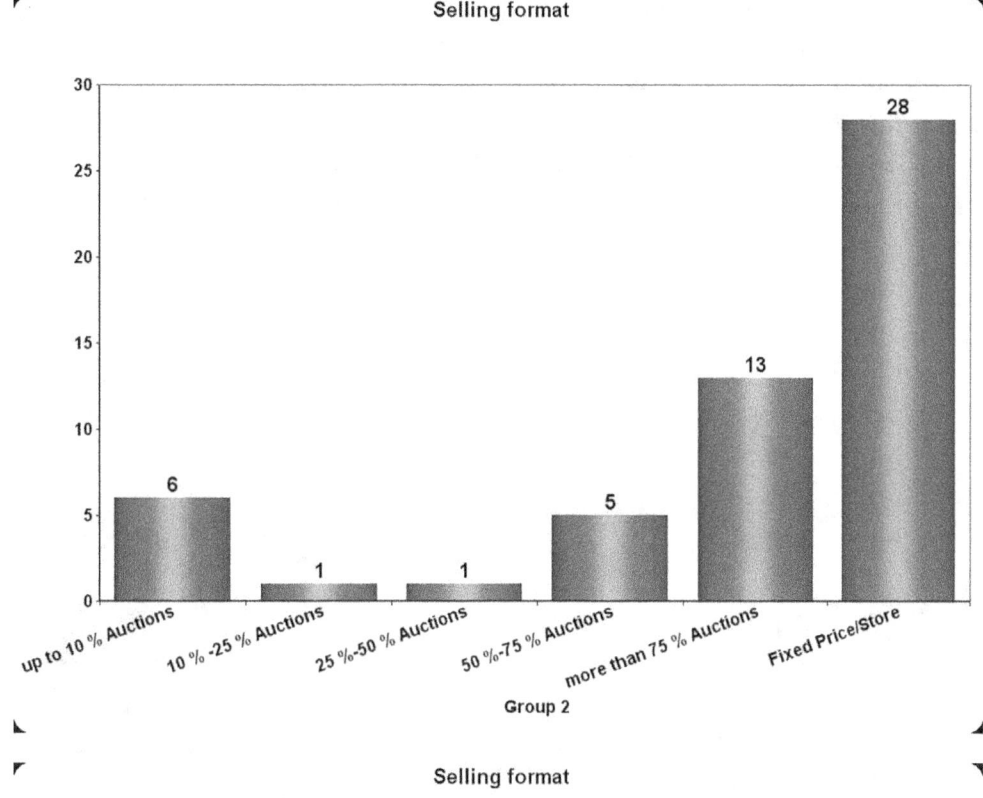

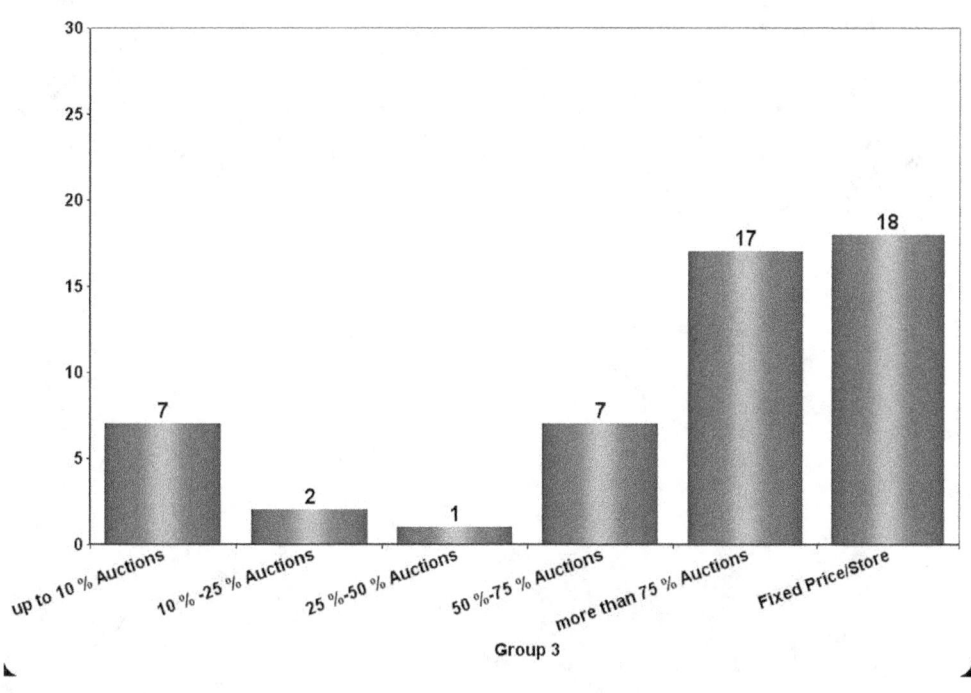

Overall, the picture comes together as follows:

44% of the 143 analyzed eBay sellers (the famous 15, which are represented in both groups 1 and 2 rather than in group 3, were counted only once as always) rely exclusively on eBay's fixed price or shop format.

56% also list in auctions, nearly 12% cautiously list in auctions and have less than 10% of listings in auctions amongst the mix of formats. Nearly 38% of sellers list more than 50% in auctions.

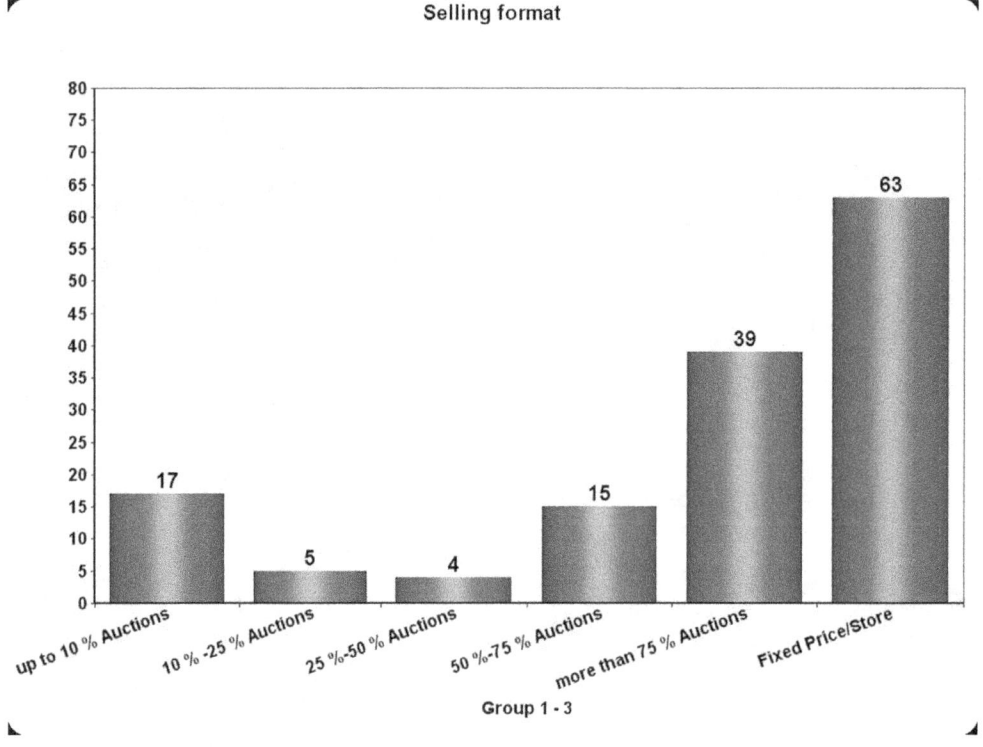

Selling format

Listing upgrades

The popular add-on option in all three groups is the additional option "subtitles".

From experience, I know that many eBay sellers are not even aware that the keywords that appear in the subtitles are not even found in classic eBay searches.

Sellers for which 80 characters in the title are not sufficient like to add the subtitles option because they want to put more keywords in their subtitles, without being clear on the fact that these keywords are not taken into account by eBay's search engine.

Keywords from the subtitles will only be displayed if the buyers' searches include the description in the advanced search.

For items that are rarely listed on eBay, a subtitle can make sense when buyers obtain too few hits from the classic search and expand the search by including the description in the search.

For the vast number of offers this will not be the case so the subtitles very often defeat the purpose they were supposed to serve.

Subtitles appear when the results of a buyer's initial search are displayed and the buyer sees the subtitle of those listings, or if they simply browse through the categories on eBay.

If you keep this in mind, you can use the extra 55 characters in your subtitles sensibly - apart from making sure to include important keywords for searches.

For example, you could conceivably add keywords such as "more than 1000x sold", "shipping within 24 hours", "shipping from the USA".

These would be additions that would not make sense to be in the title, because they do not contain important keywords.

However, in the subtitles they could act as a hook and convince a buyer to click on the item.

In deciding not to use subtitles, the three groups differ.

In the group of sellers who sell more than 30,000 items per month, over half choose to not use subtitles, whereas in the group of sellers who made sales between $500,000 and $1,000,000, only just under 25% choose not to use them, and in the group of sellers who make over $1,000,000 in sales, just 13% choose not to use subtitles.

Overall, 65% of sellers in groups 1-3 use the additional option "subtitles".

The least popular in all three groups is the listing upgrade "bold", the "second category" balanced with just under 31%, shared by all three groups. Some sellers combine additional options such as subtitles and a second category. Here is an overview:

Listing upgrades

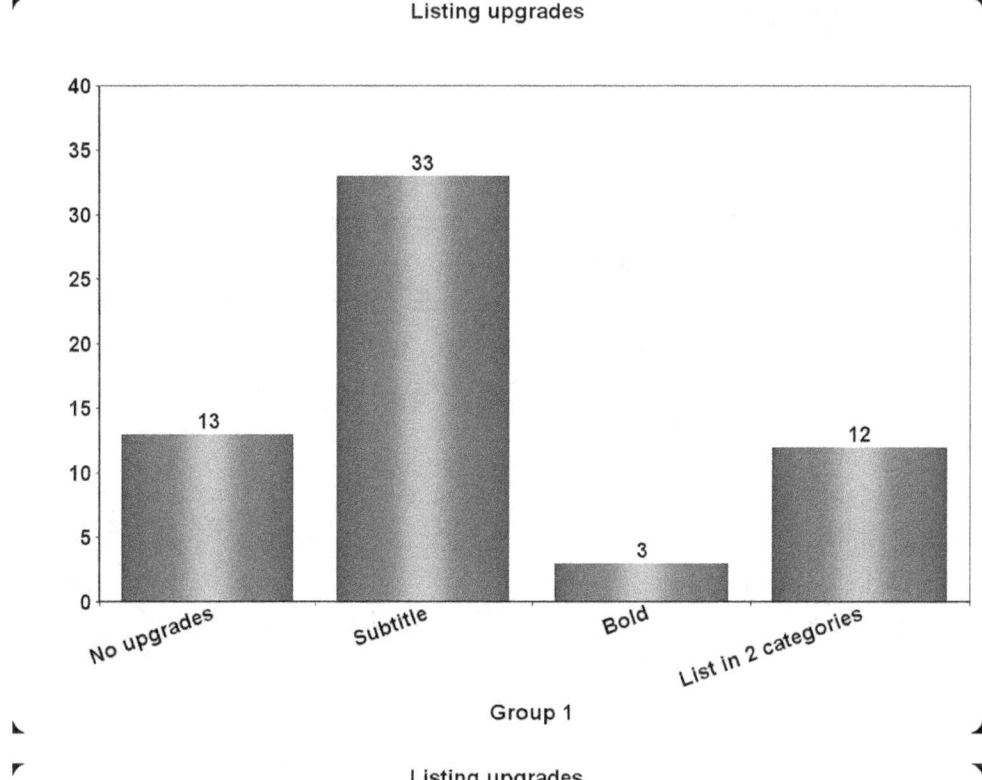

Group 1

Listing upgrades

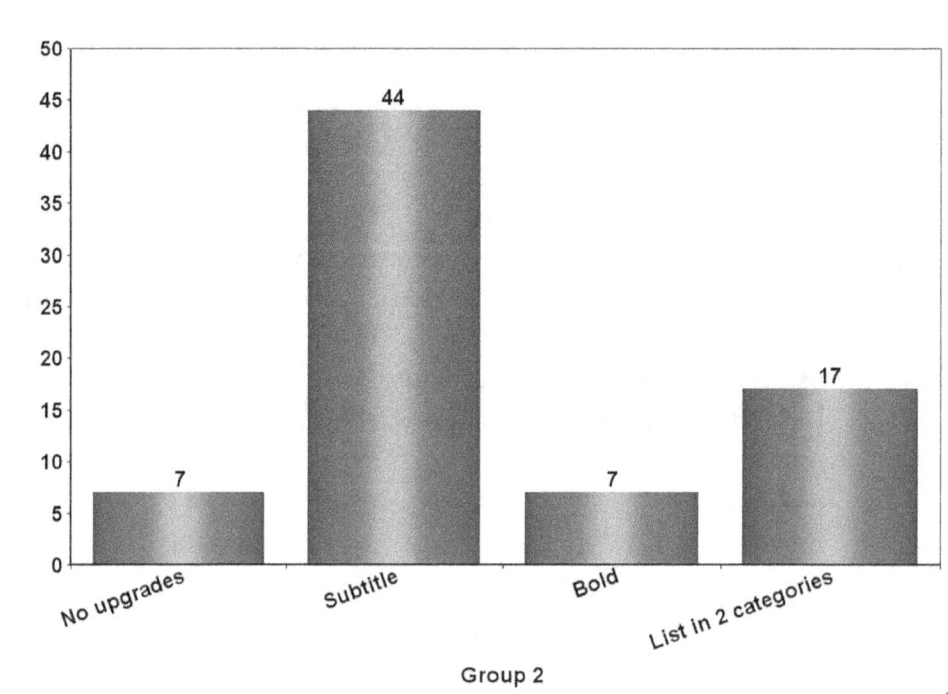

Group 2

Use of the additional options in the group 2 - over $1,000,000 in sales.

In this group, one seller stood out to me in particular, because this seller does not use the full 80 characters for the title of many listings and limits them to 20 to 30 characters, while at the same time, for some other listings, this seller selects the additional "subtitle" option.

This simply makes no sense and shows that the seller does not understand eBay.

Use of the additional options in group 3: more than 30,000 products sold.

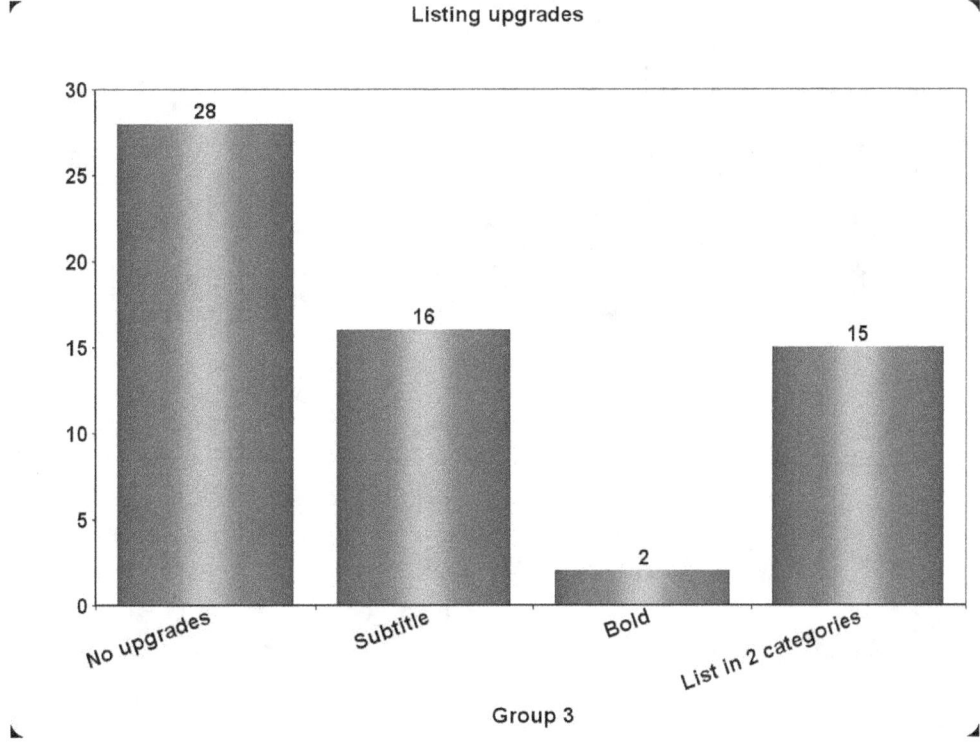

Use of the additional options in groups 1-3:

Overall, it's probably worth mentioning here that for many sellers there is much opportunity for optimization in choosing the right keywords in the title when using all 80 characters.

If they would improve here, they could save themselves the paid subtitles often booked by sellers.

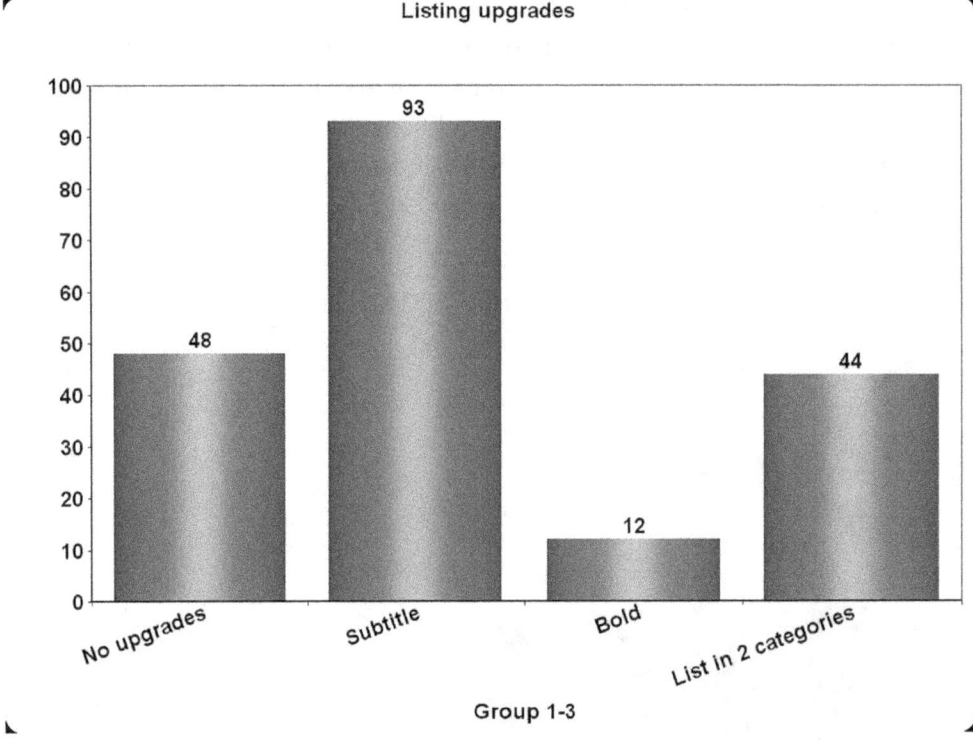

Listing upgrades

Group 1-3

Number of bids

In this relatively large proportion of auctions it is interesting to take a look at the number of bids. This analysis also includes bids that were delivered on fixed price listings, of course.

Overall, almost 7.9 million bids were placed on the offers of our 143 sellers within just one month.

Group 1 represents nearly 1.36 million bids, group 2 follows with 2.69 million bids and group 3 accounts for the lion's share with 5.7 million bids. (As always, in the overall calculation of the bids the 15 sellers who overlap in groups 1, 2 and 3 were only counted once.)

In group 1, the average is 26,000 bids that went to each individual seller. The three outliers, which received over 100,000 bids, skew the result a bit, and so the middle number falls at 10,000-25,000 bids.

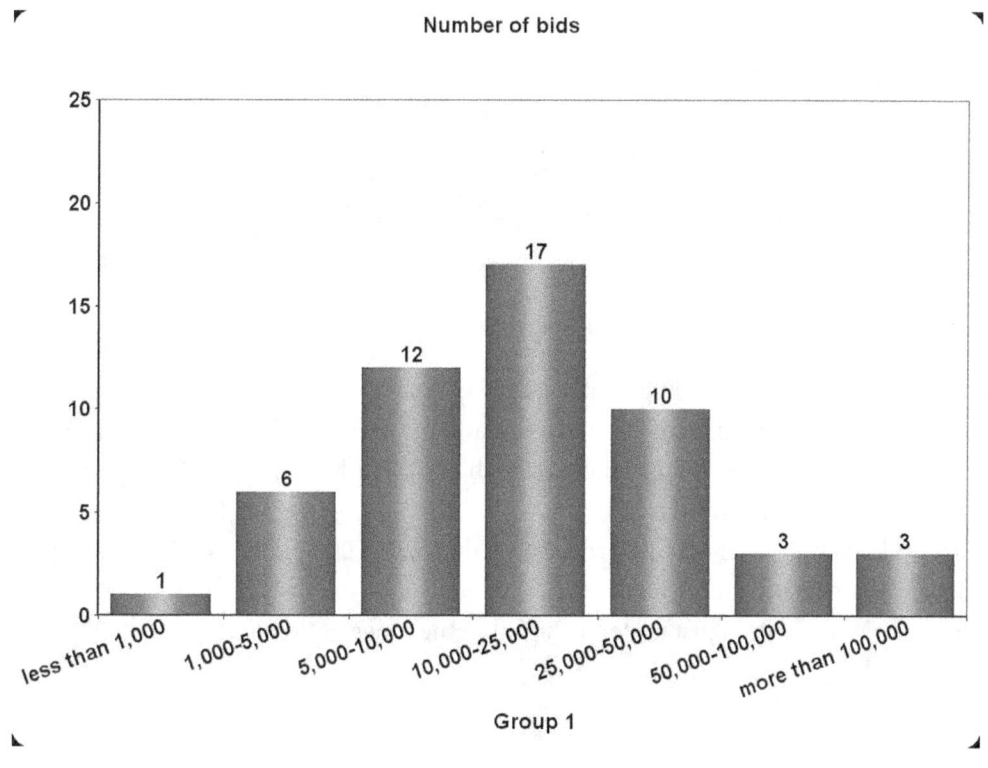

In group 2, the average is just under 50,000 bids, but here we have again four outliers whose listings received more than 100,000 bids.

Again the middle falls at just under 28% in the range of 10,000-25,000 bids, but with almost 26% followed closely by the range of 25,000-50,000.

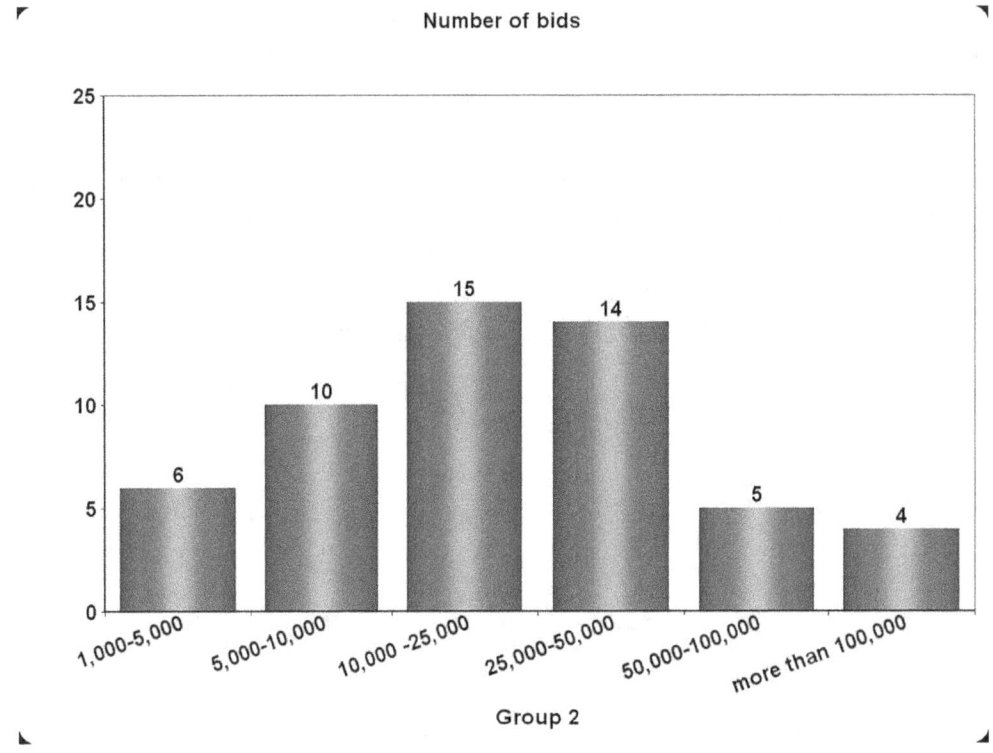

On the listings from 52 sellers in group 3, a total of nearly 5.7 million bids were submitted within one month, which would correspond to an average of just under 110,000 bids, but here we have significant upward spikes. 14 sellers were able to record more than 100,000 bids on their listings, which corresponds to almost 27%.

This group is led by a seller who recorded more than 1,035,000 bids on its listings – up to 95% of which were made in auction format.

The majority of the sellers, just under 44%, fall in the range between 25,000-50,000 bids.

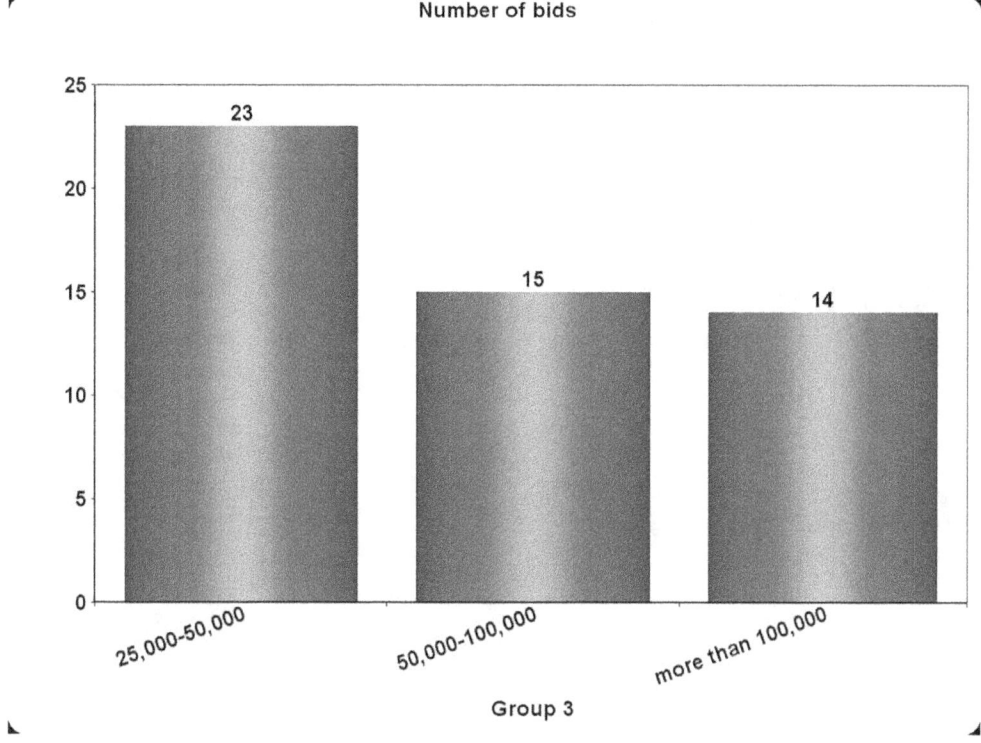

Number of bids

Group 3

Number of categories

How many of the main categories are the eBay sellers present in on eBay.com?

Do they belong more so to the "general sellers" or do they focus on a few categories?

In group 1, both ends of the scale are almost equal.

Nearly 27% of the sellers limit their listings to only one category, 25% are present in more than ten categories on eBay.com.

With almost 56%, the vast majority of sellers on eBay.com limit themselves to listings in up to three categories.

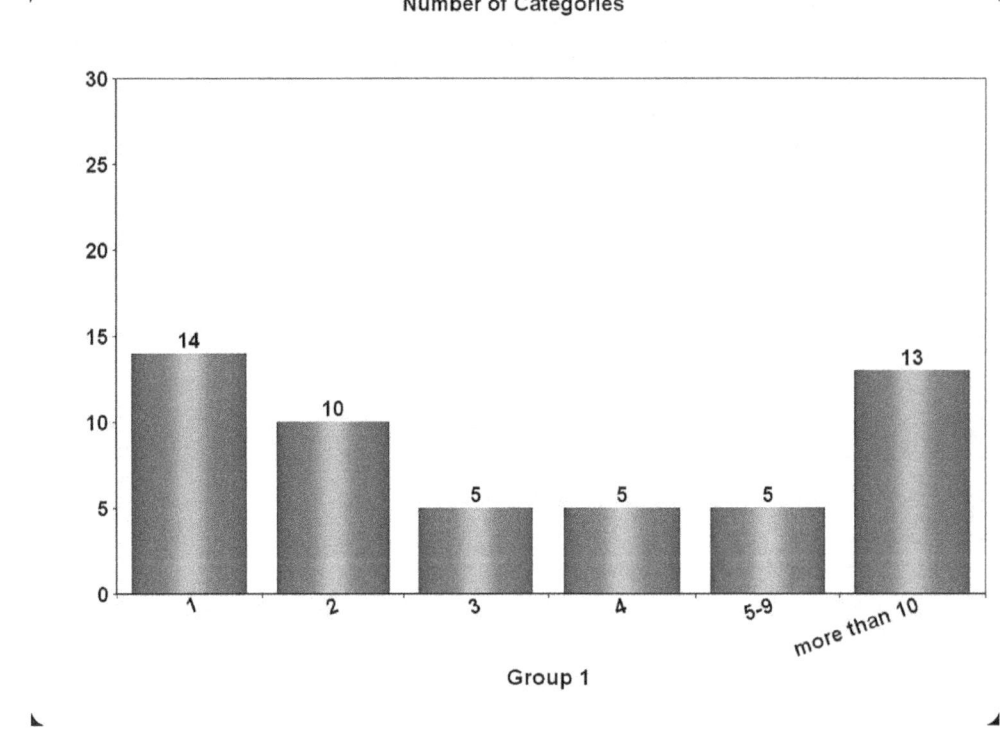

In the second group we see a somewhat different picture in the presence within categories. Here more than 52% of sellers are present in more than ten categories, but almost 35% limit themselves to presence in up to three categories on eBay.com.

In group 3, the number of sellers who are present in more than ten categories dominates the picture. With just under 54%, they make up the largest group and just 27% limit themselves to appearing in less than three categories.

Number of Categories

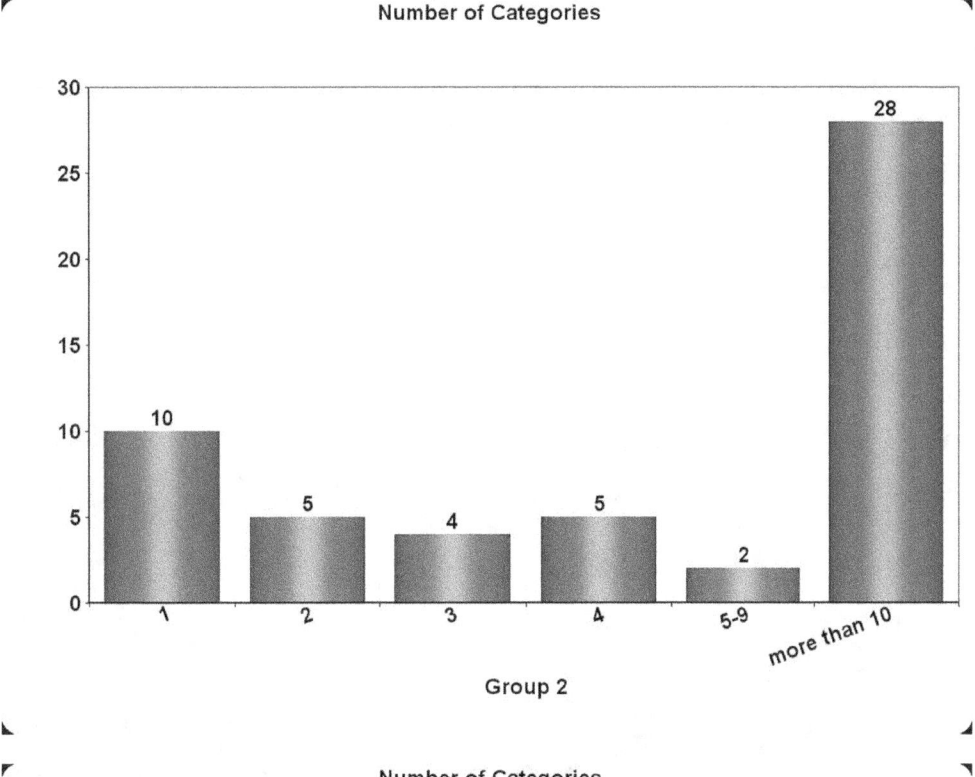

Group 2

Number of Categories

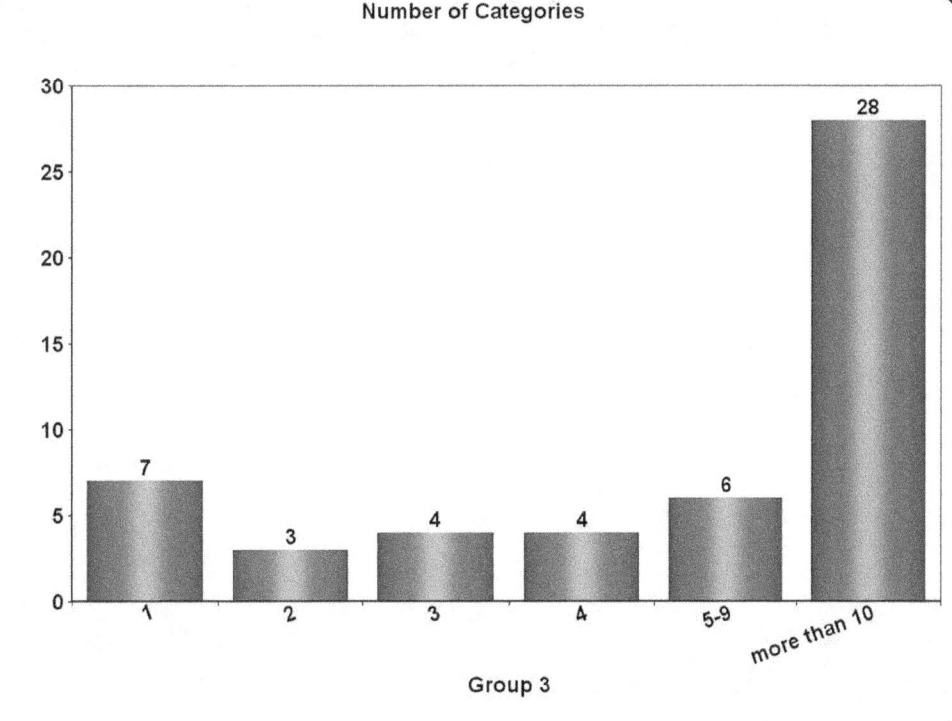

Group 3

Overall, the picture of all three groups is as follows:

The group of sellers that leads the scale with just under 41% is active in more than ten categories on eBay.com – following this comes the other end of the scale - the group of sellers that is active only in a single category, with just under 20%.

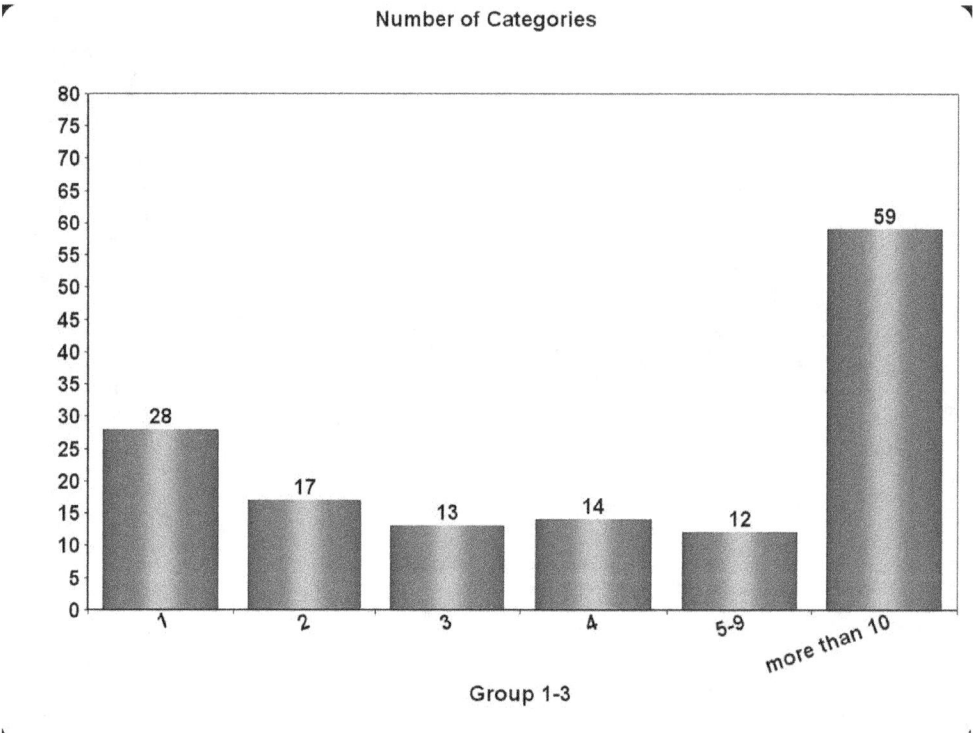

Number of Categories

Group 1-3

Listings duration - highest sale price

Now let us turn to the evaluations that are of interest to all sellers. What role does the listing duration period play in the sale prices achieved? Which duration should I choose for a listing to achieve the highest possible price?

Our 143 sellers are active in virtually every category on eBay.com. They have sold more than 3.5 million items on eBay.com in one month and should thus constitute a representative group.

Consider the relationship between the duration of the listings and selling price: in group 1, we see that the highest prices were achieved at the beginning and at the end of the scale.

21% is attributable to offers that are on eBay for one or three days, as well as shop listings that run for longer than eleven days.

Sellers who choose the listing duration period of ten days benefit the least. Here the average sale price is the lowest.

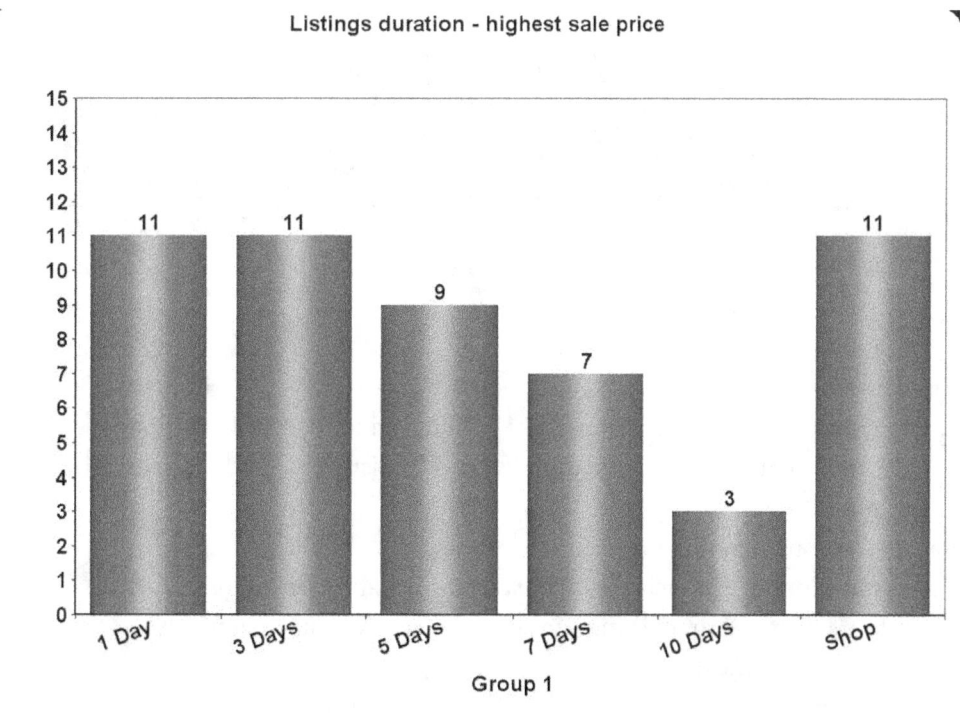

Listings duration - highest sale price

Group 1

In the second group the whole thing looks a bit different. Although here, the one-day and the shop listings lead the group with 22% each, the listing duration period of ten days follows just thereafter with 18.5% - the listing duration period, which was the least attractive in group 1.

There is no explanation for this.

The average prices in the two groups are not far from each other and the mix of categories is also similar.

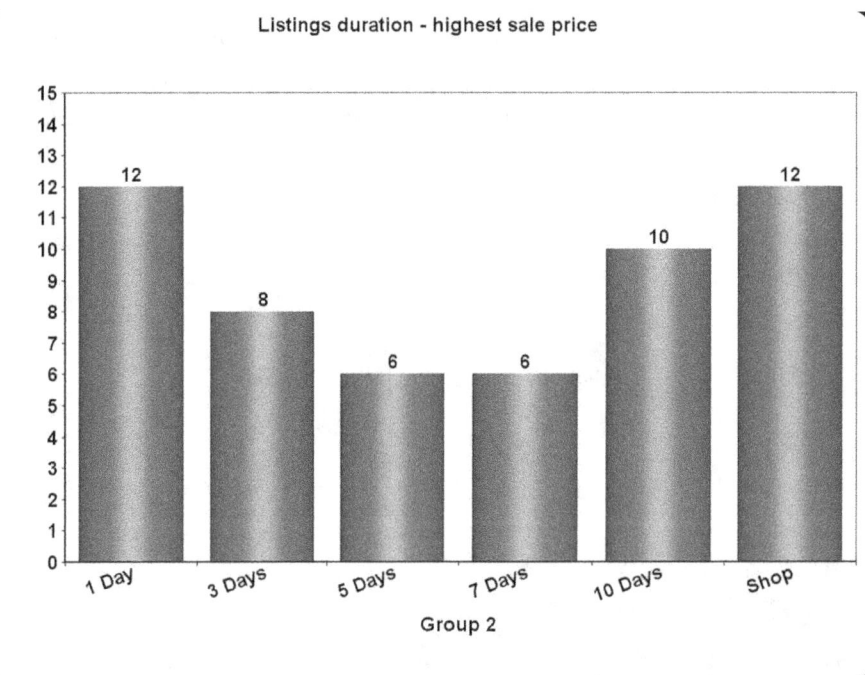

Listings duration - highest sale price

Group 2

Let's take another look at the third group:

Again, the one-day listings clearly dominate in addition to the ten-day listings and the shop listings. At the midpoint lie the three, five, and seven-day listings, slightly less than the other listing duration periods.

Overall view, the picture is as follows:

The highest sale prices were achieved with a listing duration period of more than eleven days with just under 24% on the shop listings. In second place, with just under 22%, is the listing duration period of only one day.

Listing durations of three days (16%) and ten days (14.6%) are almost equal.

In all three groups the listing duration periods of five and seven days are the least attractive, in which the selling prices are the lowest.

Listings duration - highest sale price

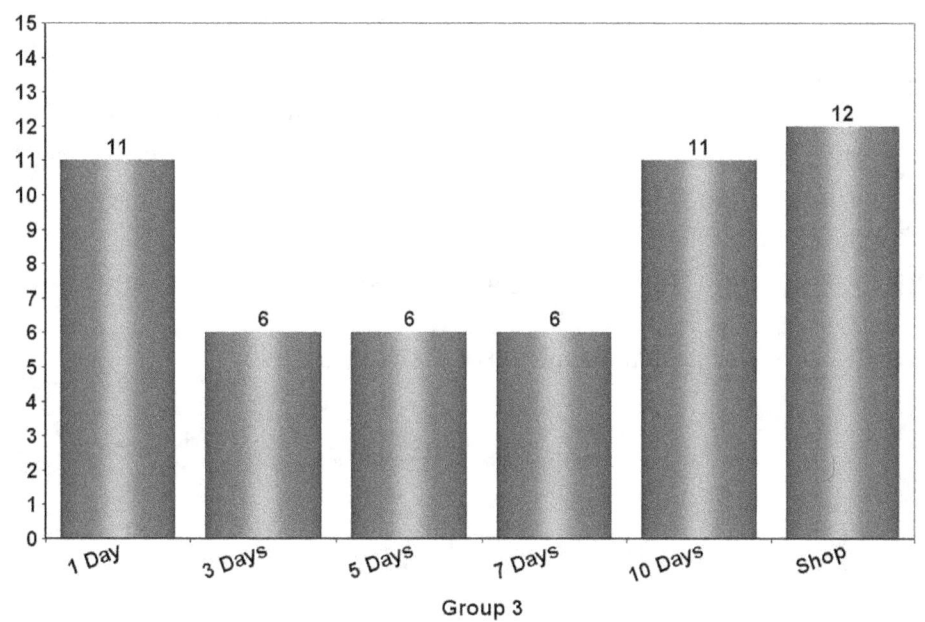

Group 3

Listings duration - highest sale price

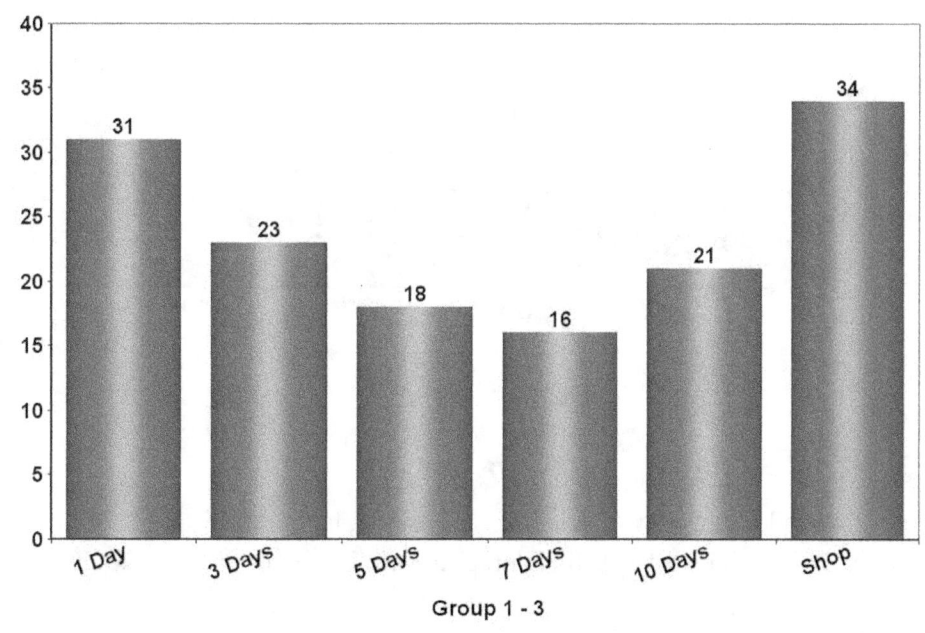

Group 1 - 3

Listing duration - highest sales quota:

Which listing duration period achieves the highest sales quota?

Which duration should I choose, therefore, to sell as many products as possible?

Unlike with the sale prices, with the sales quota several days can come into account. Many sellers choose listing duration periods of three, five and seven days, for example, and have a sales quota of 100% on each of those days.

In group 1 the shop listings with a listing duration period of more than eleven days clearly dominate.

In second place is a listing duration period of five and ten days.

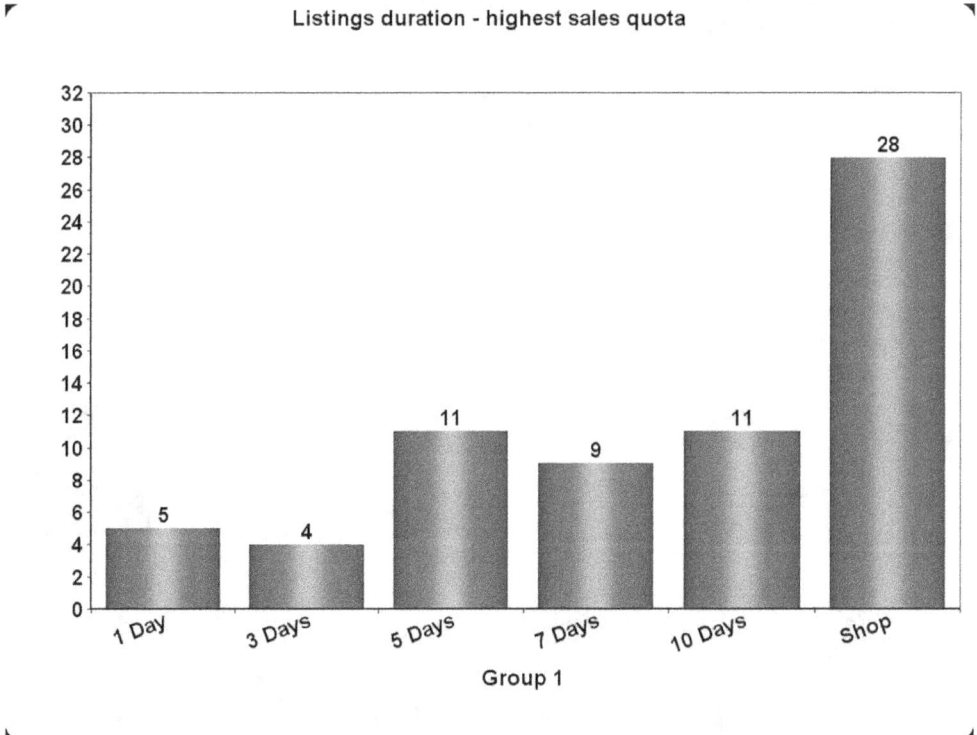

In group 2, a similar picture is shown. The clear winner here is the listing duration period of more than eleven days, followed by listing duration periods of ten and seven days.

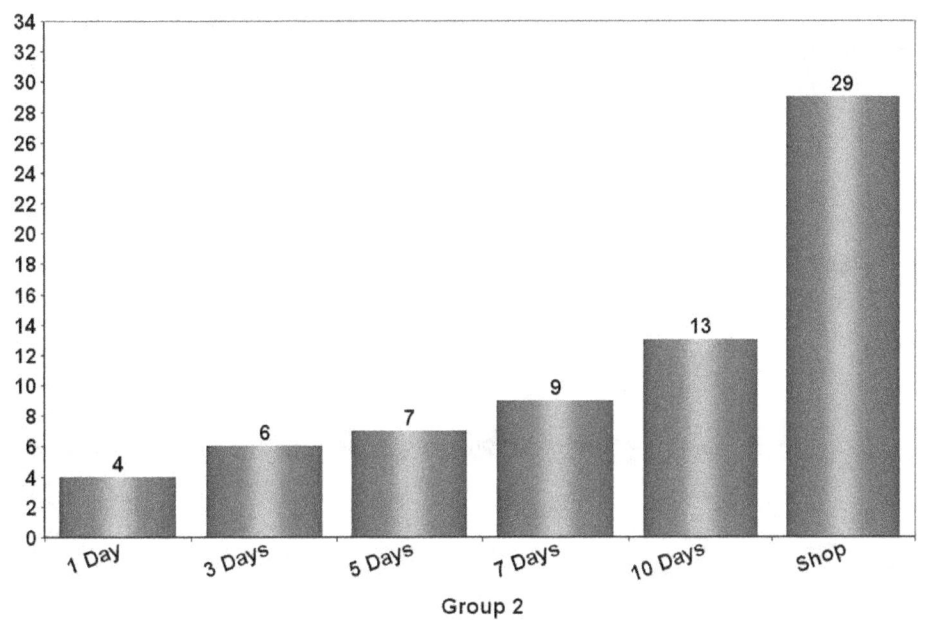

Listings duration - highest sales quota

Group 2

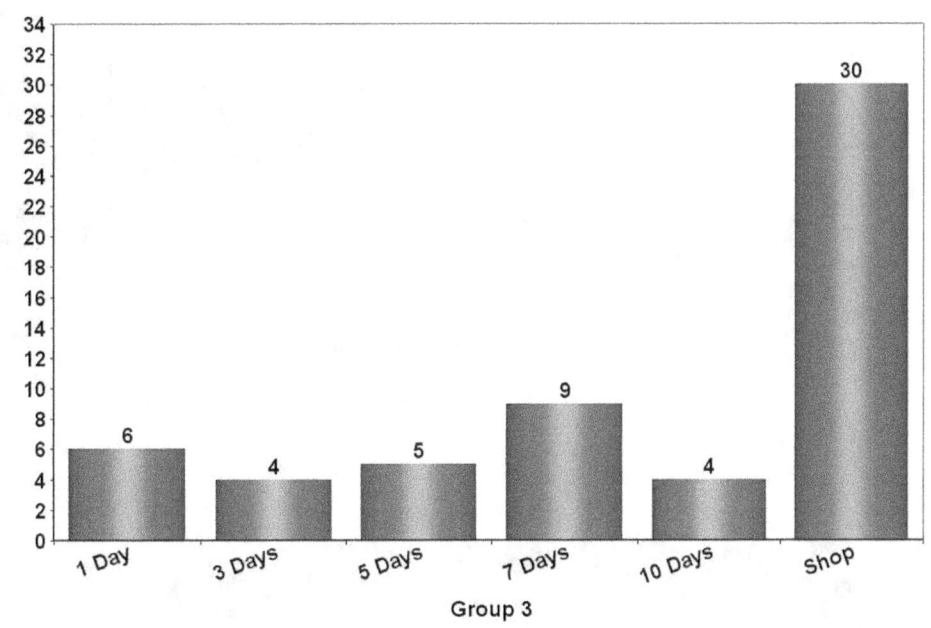

Listings duration - highest sales quota

Group 3

Also in group 3 it is confirmed that a listing duration period of more than eleven days achieves the highest sales quotas. Here, the duration of seven days comes in second place.

In the overall view this shows itself as follows:

By far the highest sales quota is achieved with a listing duration period of more than eleven days.

Then come the durations of ten days and seven days, while the duration of three days is at the bottom.

Ideally you would take the overlap between the sales price and sales quota, i.e. a listing duration in which both the highest sales prices and the highest sales rates were achieved.

This overlap is only available with listing duration periods of more than eleven days, i.e. with shop listings.

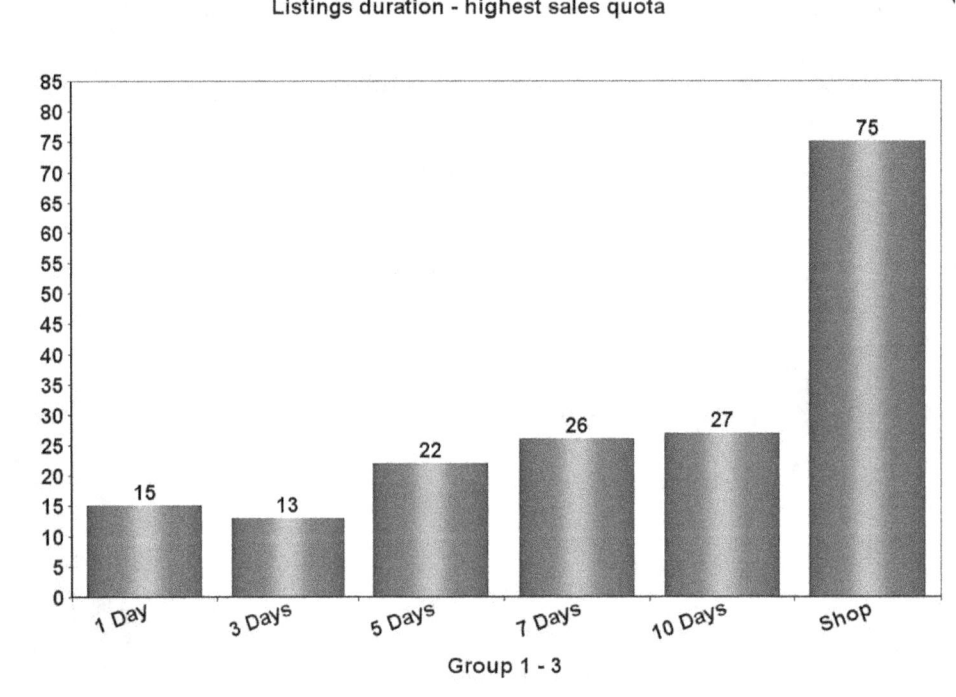

Listings duration - highest sales quota

Group 1 - 3

Highest sales prices by day

The question that I get asked the most is the question of which day is the best day for selling on eBay.

For years, the rumor has continued that Sunday is the best day to let eBay listings expire.

First you have to define what is meant by the "best day", because there are two figures. The first figure refers to the highest price, the second to the highest sales quota.

On what day are the highest prices achieved and on what day are the most items sold on eBay?

If one thinks about it, it quickly becomes clear that the intersection will be low here. On days when many items are sold, the selling prices will be lower than on days when fewer items are sold. The evaluations will confirm this shortly.

Traditionally, Sunday is actually a good day on eBay, because many people have time and are active on the Internet, but is it actually worth it to have listings expire on Sunday on eBay? Let's explore this question in more detail:

When evaluating the highest sale prices it's shown in group 1 that on Tuesday and Wednesday the highest prices are achieved, while the prices go down drastically on weekends.

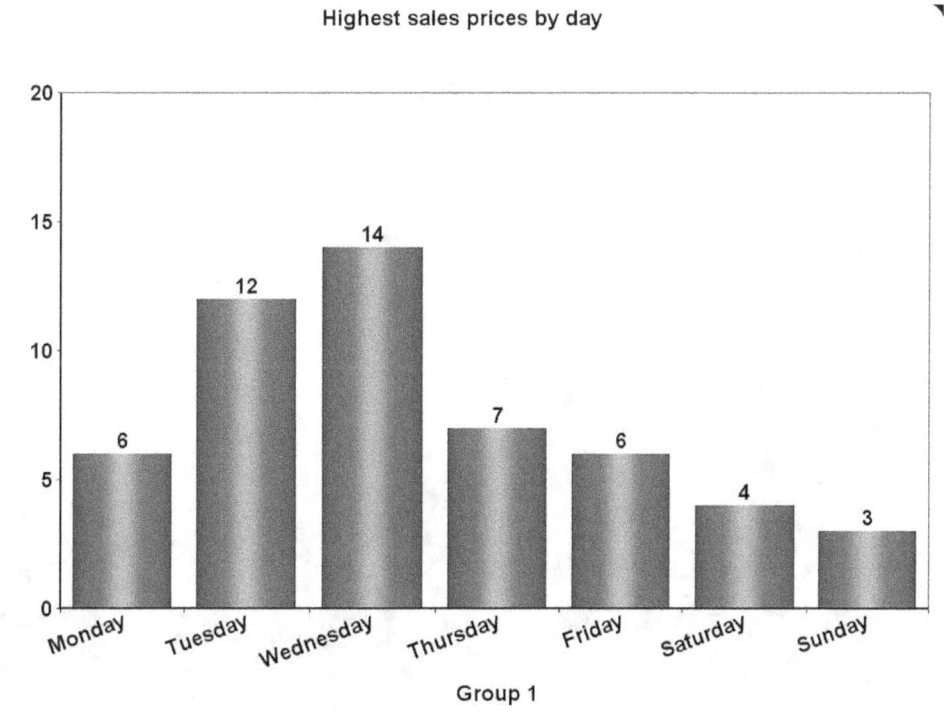

Highest sales prices by day

Group 1

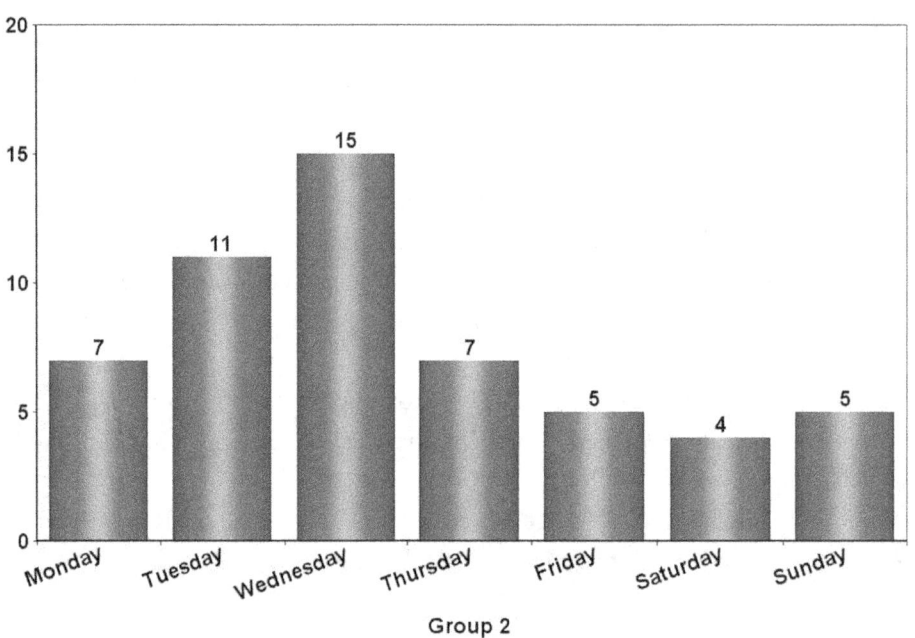

Highest sales prices by day

Group 2

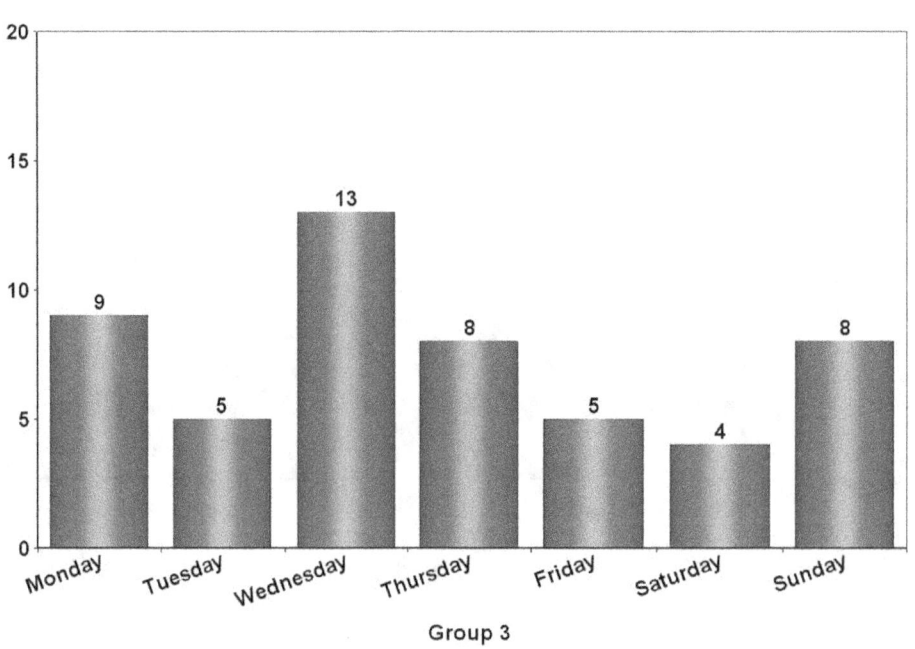

Highest sales prices by day

Group 3

THE LARGEST SELLERS ON EBAY.COM

And a look at group 2 confirms this picture. Again, Tuesday and Wednesday are the days that see the highest sales prices while the weekend is at the other end of the scale.

And also in group 3, Wednesday shows itself as the day when the highest sale prices were obtained. Here, the second strongest day is Monday, a weekday.

In the overall view it's clear: in all three groups, Wednesday leads with almost 25% as the day on which the highest sale price is achieved. Tuesday then follows with 17.5%, and Monday with just 15.5%. Far behind at the end of the scale are Saturday and Sunday, the days on which the second lowest selling prices are achieved.

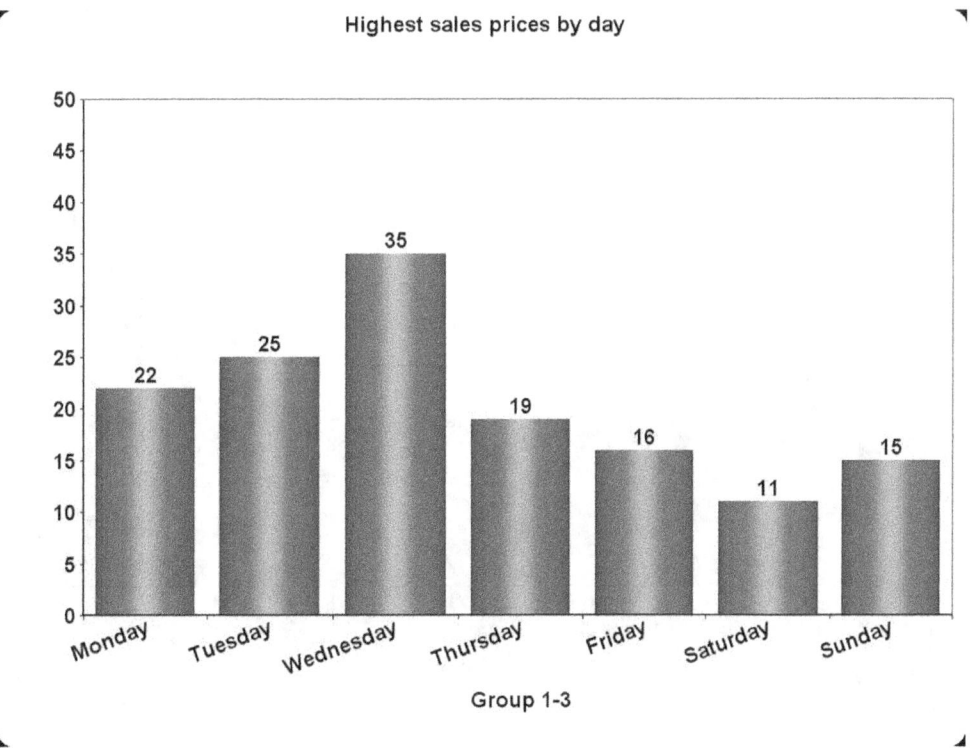

Highest sales prices by day

Group 1-3

Highest sales prices by day | 63

Highest sales quota per day

Now let's take a look at the sales quota. On what days are the most items sold on eBay?

Again, unlike with the sale prices, several days can come into account with the sales quota, so here we see the total numbers in the analysis higher than that of the sale price.

In group 1 we land on the weekend. Sunday is the day when most of the products are sold on eBay, followed closely by Saturday.

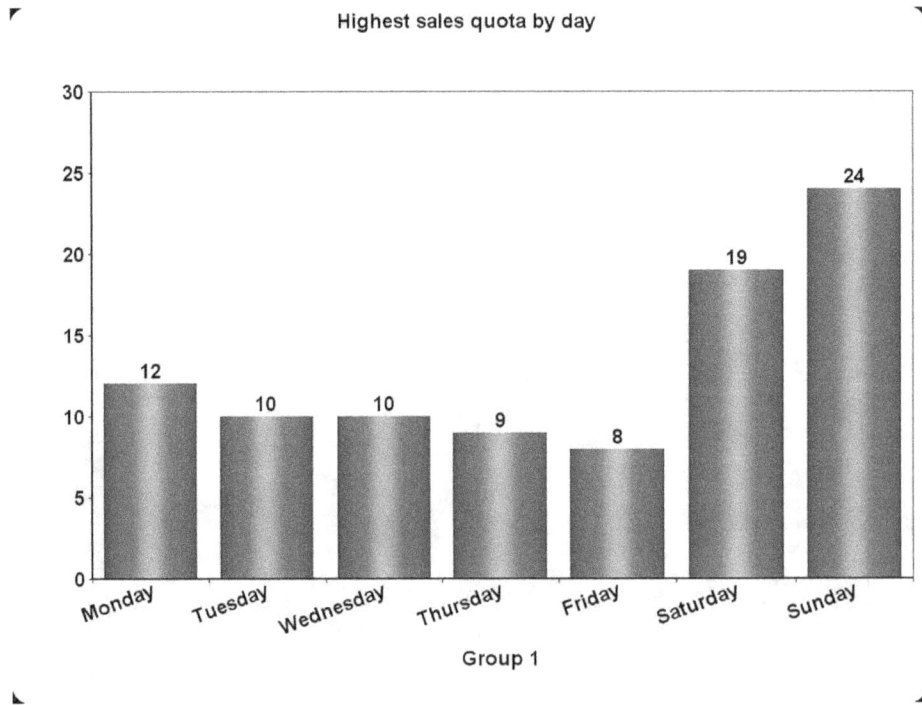

Highest sales quota by day

This is also confirmed in group 2.

Sunday is the strongest selling day, followed closely by Saturday, while the weekdays fall much farther down the lineup.

In group 3, the outliers are not quite so enormous, but here Sunday is the day on which the most items are sold, while Saturday follows as the second strongest sales day.

The other days are not so far behind, but this is certainly due to the average selling prices in this group that are significantly below the average selling prices of the other two groups. In this group the rather inexpensive "convenience items" are sold that buyers put into their shopping carts and purchase without much thought.

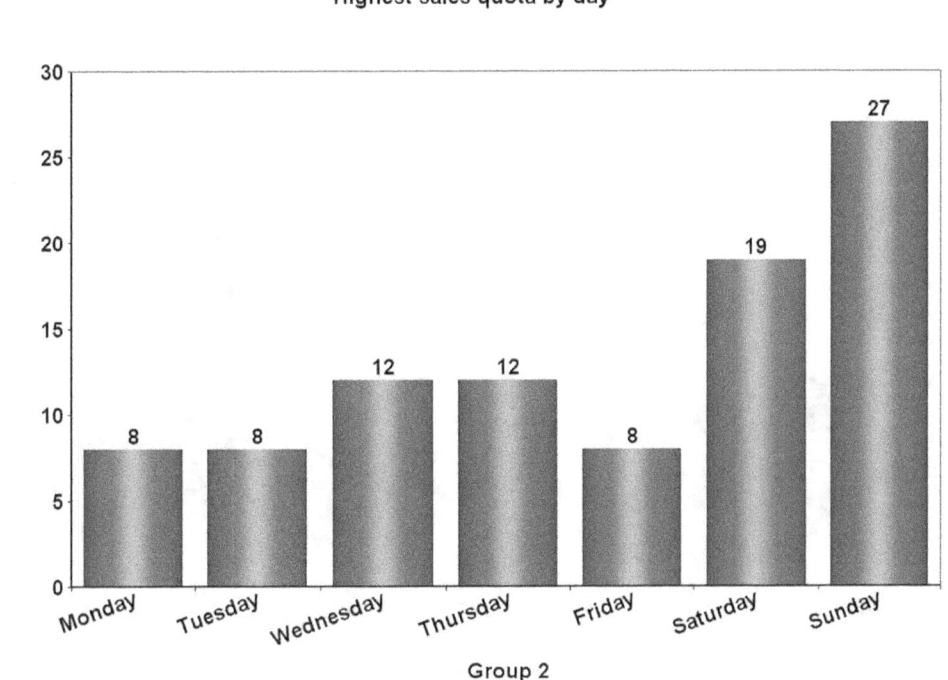

Highest sales quota by day

Group 2

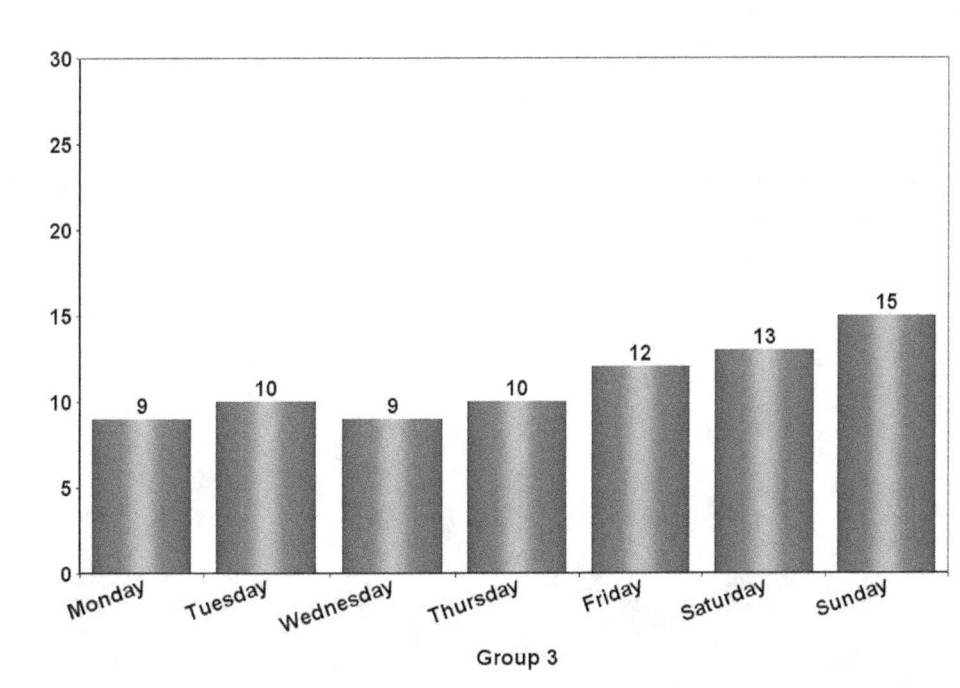

Highest sales quota by day

Group 3

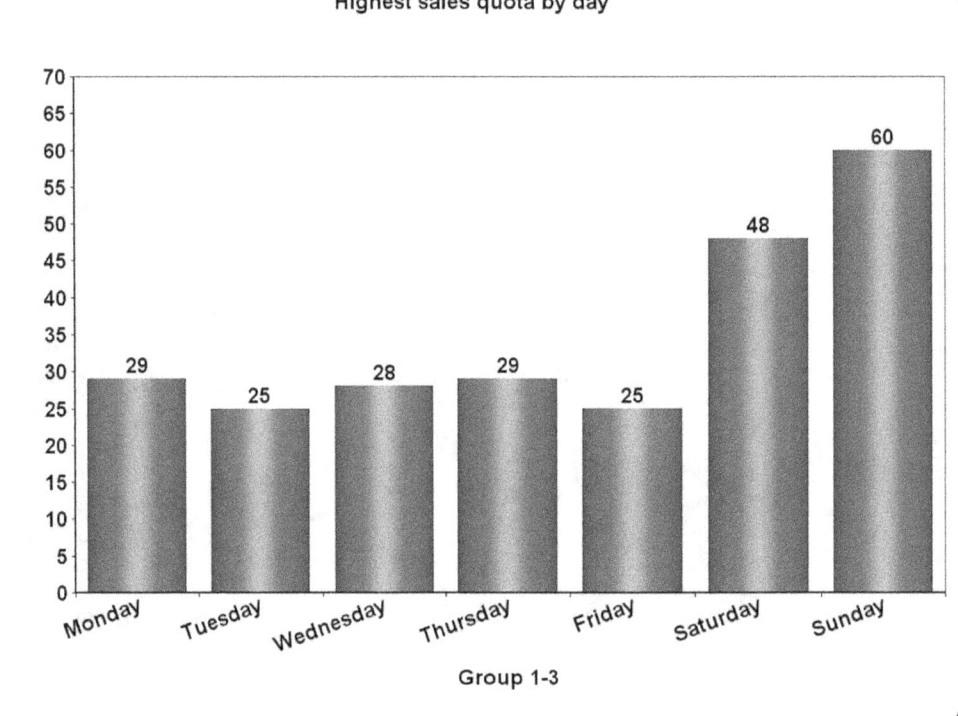

In the overall picture, the result is as follows:

Sunday differs significantly from all other days, when it comes to the number of items sold, and even Saturday clearly lies ahead of the weekdays.

As expected there is no overlap to be found in the days when the highest sale prices were achieved. On eBay.com many items are sold on the weekend; the highest prices are achieved, however, on Tuesday and Wednesday.

Most expensive items

Now we come to some other numbers that surprised me, in part.

What price range included the most expensive items that eBay sellers sold on eBay.com?

In group 1, the majority of sellers ranging between $500 and $1,000, but overall there is also quite a lot of movement between $1,000 and $10,000. The most expensive item sold in this group was a ring at a price of $28,600.09.

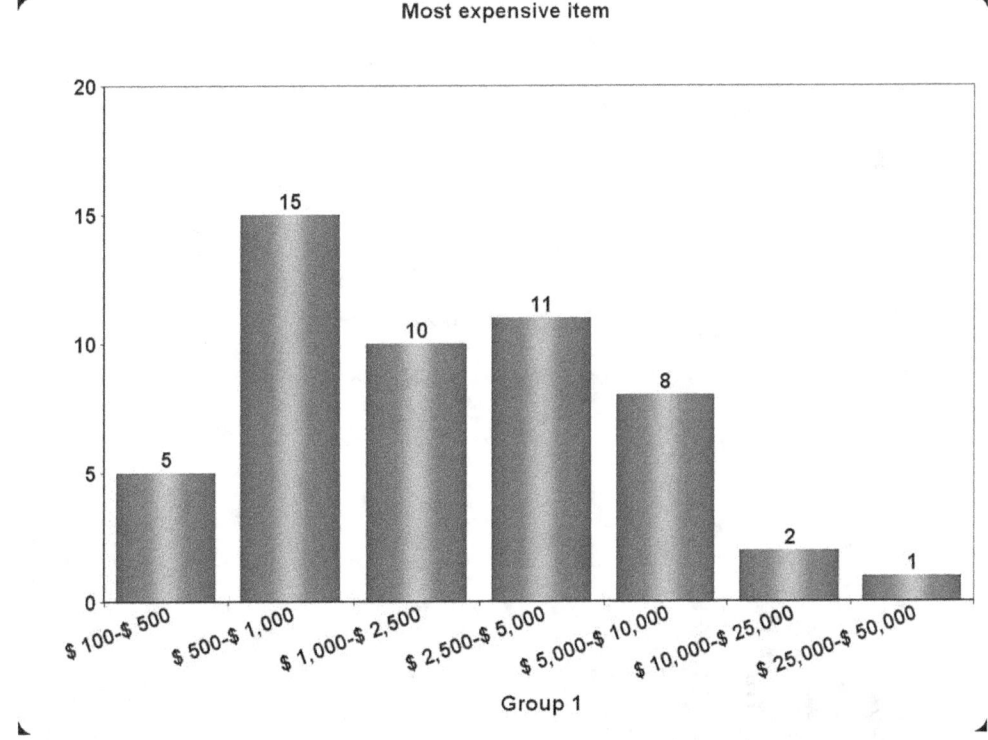

Most expensive item

Group 1

In the second group we see an increase over the first.

Here the most expensive items sold are in the range between $2,500 and $5,000, but here it also shows that the vast majority of sellers fall in the range between $1,000 and $10,000.

In this group we had three listings that almost took my breath away.

The most expensive item in this group was similar to group 1, a ring that sold for $4,000,000; in second place was another ring with a sale price of $555,000.

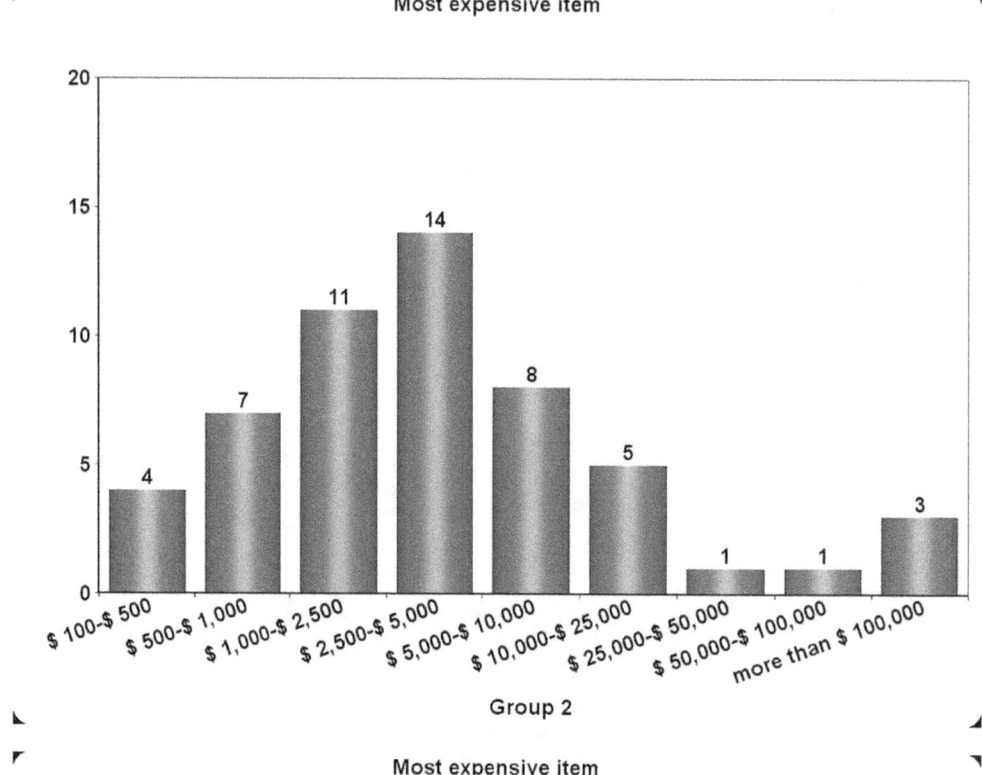

Most expensive item

Group 2

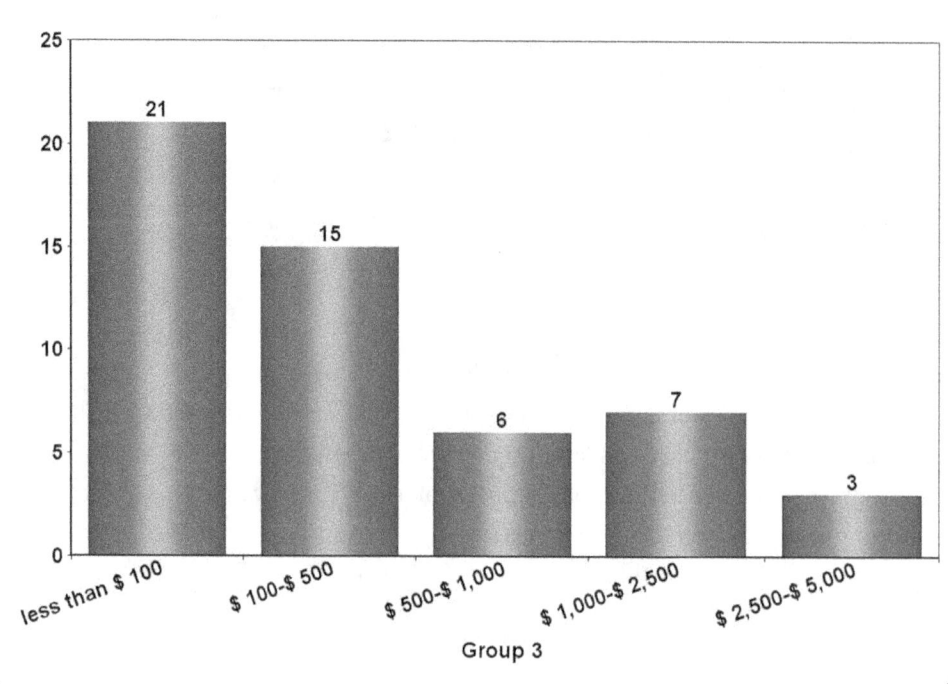

Most expensive item

Group 3

Both listings looked to me very realistic, so I have taken them into account within the analysis. The sellers have significant ratings in their profiles on eBay.com and they regularly sell jewelry in these price ranges, which one would not necessarily think to find on eBay.

The third item, which was sold for more than $100,000, was a tractor. This is also an item where I would not necessarily think of eBay as a sales platform for it, but in this case my assessment was wrong. Tractors and excavators are sold successfully and in considerable quantities on eBay.com.

In group 3, the situation is almost sad. For 40% of the sellers, the most expensive item sold went for less than $100; the most expensive item sold in this group overall was sold at $4,402.99.

Bestsellers

Finally, we will take a look at the bestselling items that the sellers analyzed have sold:

8.545 x Multi Task Utility Work Gloves

8.431 x SWAT BW8202 XM-L T6 3W CREE 120 Lumens LED Flashlight

7.592 x Ray-Ban Sunglasses

6.680 x Hard Back Case for Apple iPhone

6.527 x NY Hotel Deluxe 300TC Cotton Bed Sheet Set

5.282 x Apple iPad Mini 32 GB

5.112 x Hotel Comfort Bamboo Memory Foam Pillow with Bag

4.739 x eBay Gift Card

4.706 x USB Home AC Wall Charger + 8 Pin Data Sync Cable Cord for iPhone 5

4.644 x Pocket Hose The Hose That Grows To 50 ft

4.439 x USB Home AC Wall + Car Charger + 2 x 8 Pin Data Sync Cable For iPhone

4.149 x USB Data Cable Sync Cord+AC Power Wall Charger for iPhone 4

3.603 x Apple Lightning to USB Charge & Sync Cable for iPhone 5S

3.439 x 10 oz Scottsdale STACKER® Silver Bar - Ten Troy oz .999 Silver Bullion

3.228 x Latest Version iPad Mini with Retina Display

3.177 x 2014 1 oz Silver American Eagle (Lot of 10)

3.109 x 8GB iRulu 7" Android 4.0 Tablet

2.995 x Adidas Golf Shoes

2.873 x 64 GB Lexar JumpDrive USB 3.0 High Speed Flash Drive

2.809 x Lenovo 10.1" Windows 8 Tablet 2

2.724 x PlayStation 4 Console

2.663 x Asus Google Nexus 7 Tablet 16 GB

2.416 x Manufacturer Refurbished 64 GB Microsoft Surface RT Tablet

2.215 x Ray-Ban Large Aviator Sunglasses

2.134 x Rotating Tie Rack

2.120 x Lexar JumpDrive TwistTurn 16 GB USB 2.0 Flash Drive 4 Pack

2.047 x Apple iPhone 5S 16 GB

2.044 x Apple iPad Air 32 GB

2.040 x Lot of 5 - 2014 1 Troy Oz .999 Fine Silver American Eagle Coins

1.992 x G.SKILL 64GB MicroSDXC Flash Card

1.921 x Patio Umbrella

1.900 x Iphone 5

1.692 x Zero Gravity Chairs Case Of (2)

1.673 x Call of Duty: Ghosts for Microsoft Xbox One

1.545 x Samsung Galaxy S III

1.500 x Sony PlayStation 4 500 GB

1.500 x Wii U 32 GB

1.495 x Amazon Kindle Fire HDX 7" Tablet

1.411 x Battlefield 4: Standard Edition (PlayStation 4)

1.303 x Dell XPS 12 Touchscreen 2-in-1 (i5) 128 GB SSD 12.5" Ultrabook

1.364 x Vera Bradley Zip-Around Wallet

1.346 x Western Digital Elements 2TB Portable External Hard Drive

1.340 x Lot 2 Wireless Controller Bluetooth for Sony PS3

1.336 x 3.5mm Earphone Headset for Apple iPhone 5 4/4S

1.330 x 5x 10oz Scottsdale STACKER® Silver Bars 50 Troy oz .999 Silver Bullion

1.304 x Apple Macbook Pro

1.271 x Replacement Assembly for iPhone 4S

1.200 x Sony PlayStation 4 / PS4 Console

1.002 x Replacement Assembly for iPod Touch

992 x Apple iPhone 4s – 16 GB

970 x SilverTowne Logo 1oz .999 Fine Silver Bar LOT OF 10

826 x Canon EOS-M Mirrorless Digital Camera

672 x Ladies Complete Golf Club Set

881 x Lenovo IdeaTab

803 x Dell Inspiron M731R 17.3" HD+ Notebook

599 xGoogle Chromecast HDMI Streaming Media Player

592 x Adidas Golf Shorts

586 x (2) Game Spy Low Glow Infrared Digital Trail Hunting Cameras

465 x Nikon D3200 24.2 MP CMOS Digital SLR Camera with 18-55mm VR Lens Refurbished

453 x Full Body Shiatsu Massage Chair

438 x Taylormade 2014 Jetspeed Driver

417 x Dell Alienware 14" HD Gaming Notebook

406 x Natural Chemistry PHOSFREE Swimming Pool Phosphate Remover

399 x Folding Electric Treadmill Portable Motorized Running Machine

342 x Google - Chromecast HDMI Streaming Media Playe

354 x Invicta Mens Specialty Chronograph

239 x Horse Head Mask Latex

234 x Royal Canadian Mint RCM 1 Troy Oz .9999 Gold Bar

216 x Barber Chair

190 x Samsung UN65F8000 - 65 inch 1080p 240hz 3D Smart Wifi LED HDTV

129 x Mirrors Pair for 99-02 Chevy GMC Truck

33 x Rolex Submariner

20 x Mens Rolex Datejust Watch

1 x Cartier 2.66ct GIA Princess Cut Diamond Platinum Engagement Ring for $28,600.09

1 x 1953 Topps Mickey Mantle SHORT PRINT for $ 23.650,99

1 x 18.2 Ct Carat Round Cut Engagement Solitaire Diamond Ring for $555,000

1 x GIA Certified 62.12 ct FLAWLESS Paraiba Tourmaline Diamond for $4,000,000

Overall, the following products are among the bestsellers from the sellers analyzed:

- Golf accessories from golf clubs to golf clothes to range finders
- Cameras
- Camcorder
- Books
- Coins
- Gold and silver bars
- Jewelry, watches and precious stones
- Smart Watches
- Household appliances such as refrigerators and stoves
- Computers, laptops & tablets, as well as the full range of accessories
- Smartphones & accessories
- E-book readers
- Men's toys such as helicopters, flying platforms and accessories
- Consoles and Accessories
- Computer games
- Musical instruments such as saxophones, electric guitars
- Swimming pools and accessories such as sand filters, chlorine tablets
- Kitchen gadgets such as ice cream makers, coffee machines
- Construction equipment such as tractors and hydraulic shovels and accessories
- Bags in all varieties, from handbags to backpacks
- Sports equipment such as treadmills
- Packaging materials such as envelopes, bubble wrap and tape
- Label printers
- Speakers
- Headphones
- eBay gift cards
- Bed covers, pillows and bed linen

- Collectibles like baseball cards, fan memorabilia
- Auto Parts
- Clothing and accessories, especially sunglasses
- TV sets
- Wall mounts
- Monitors
- Printers
- Garden furniture from garden hoses to garden umbrellas to outdoor furniture
- Garden tools such as hedge trimmers
- Grills
- Air conditioners and fans
- Massage chairs
- Spy cameras
- DVDs, Blue-Ray discs, videos, CDs
- Dust masks
- Work gloves
- Knives in many variations
- Insect repellent
- LED lamps of all kinds
- Media players
- Hard drives
- USB memory sticks and memory cards
- USB cables
- Modems
- Batteries
- Battery chargers
- Storage items such as boxes or tie racks
- Zippos
- Pet supplies such as dog kennels or cages
- DJ Equipment
- GPS navigation systems
- Calculators
- Hunting accessories
- Mattresses
- Sewing machines
- Tents

- Scales, especially gold scales
- Makeup kits and brushes
- Manicure Sets
- Tattoo machines
- Holster

Afterword

Although the analyzed sellers play in the top of the eBay league, in almost all areas they are a very heterogeneous group.

This becomes clear, for example, with average prices ranging between $0.76 and $122,697, and also with feedback scores that have between 1,162 and 3,896,406 ratings. This continues with the number of items listed, the number of items sold, and the number of bids.

But that's exactly what makes the evaluation so interesting, because it covers a very wide range of different sellers, thus enabling a comprehensive view of the eBay marketplace.

Overall, however, some results have to be examined critically.

Is it desirable, for example, to sell more than 30,000 items at an average price of $0.76 on eBay? I don't think so.

For one seller who sells used smartphones, I was very surprised at the numbers attributed to it. The seller has only been registered since May 2014 on eBay and in July 2014, it had nearly 8,000 sales, which already generated revenue of just under $ 2.8 million. In reality this should not be possible, because new sellers on eBay get a sales limit. Here, it does not seem to have been the case.

This seller's profile ratings, at 95.5%, are some of the worst ratings of all the sellers analyzed. With this one, I had actually expected the seller to no longer be there when I finished the book, but it is still active, but eBay seems to have now imposed a limit because its sales have fallen to just under $78,000.

Certainly there are many sellers on eBay.com who have flown under the radar with my first overview because they have not made it into the league of sales millionaires, nor do they belong to the high-volume sellers and yet, they come out better in terms of their bottom line compared to some of the sellers analyzed here.

Revenue does not just mean earnings, and also the number of ratings says nothing about whether a seller on eBay is really successful.

On the other hand, the evaluation also shows the potential that exists on eBay.com and that not all of the sellers who play in the big leagues are out of your reach. On the contrary: some may be better off if they would improve their listings. And also, if you take a look, you'll see that eBay newcomers are among the sellers analyzed, proof that you can still start successfully on eBay and leave your competitors in the dust.

That being said, I'd like to wish all eBay sellers success!

Conclusion

The evaluations were carefully created with the help of the eBay marketplace research tool Terapeak.

Reporting period: mid-June 2014 to the end of July 2014.

About the author

Marion von Kuczkowski started her career in 1999 at eBay USA and, as one of the first Germans to do so, received PowerSeller status in the same year. In 2000, Ms. von Kuczkowski was recorded as the first German in the eBay elite, the circle of the top 500 sellers in the world (today PESA). In 2002 she wrote the first German book about eBay, "Power Selling with eBay", and in 2004 she wrote the "eBay Pocket Guide". Both books were bestsellers.

From 2002 to 2007, Marion von Kuczkowski was an external eBay trainer at eBay Universities, for eBay Live and for many Chamber of Commerce workshops on eBay. Since 2002, she has advised and guided businesses and PowerSellers in their activities on eBay. In 2006, she was the initiator of the world's first product launch on all global eBay marketplace throughout the world.

Bibliography:

[*1]Source: Tamebay.com
http://tamebay.com/2011/08/ebay-38-of-sales-come-from-a-few-top-sellers.html